THANK YOU,
WODEHOUSE

THANK YOU, WODEHOUSE

BY J. H. C. MORRIS

WITH CONTRIBUTIONS BY
A. D. MACINTYRE

INTRODUCTION BY
FRANCES DONALDSON

ST. MARTIN'S PRESS
NEW YORK

827
Mo

1. Wodehouse, P.G. – Criticism
2. Wit and humor, English
I. Title

~~Library of Congress Number~~

ISBN 0-312-79494-0

First Edition

CONTENTS

Authors' note

These essays were written six years ago, in the intervals between more important work, purely for the amusement of our friends and with no thought of publication. Thanks to the kindness of Frances Donaldson, they are now revised and brought up to date and offered to a wider public. We owe a deep debt of gratitude to Frances Donaldson, not only for making publication possible but also for writing such a gay and charming Introduction.

We are grateful to the trustees of the Wodehouse estate for giving us permission to quote from his works.

'The critic Howarth' who is referred to more than once in these pages is the oldest friend of one of us and has been a Wodehouse fan for longer than either of us. We are grateful to him for much stimulating correspondence and conversation about Wodehouse.

All of the pages that follow are the work of J.H.C.M. except the addenda at the end of chapters 2 and 4 and chapter 3, section 2, which were written by A.D.M.

J.H.C.M.
A.D.M.

INTRODUCTION

This book is published as a tribute to P.G. Wodehouse on the hundredth anniversary of his birth, and it comes, as is most appropriate, from Oxford.

Wodehouse himself laid down the rule that an author should give his qualifications for introducing a book. Slightly surprised at finding myself introducing the work of two Oxford dons, I hasten to explain how this unexpected turn of events came about. (Any writer well-versed in Wodehouse may use an occasional cliché as an allusion.)

In the first place, I am merely the intermediary through whom the manuscript reached the publishers. Hearing that I was at work on a biography of P.G. Wodehouse, Dr Morris and Dr Macintyre sent me their manuscripts with no thought in their minds other than that they might be of use to me. Immediately realising that these were contributions of high quality and worthy of better things than mere quotation in someone else's book, I loaned them, with the authors' permission, to my publisher. Negotiations followed, resulting in the publication of this book, which will come not merely as an anniversary tribute to Wodehouse, but, one may feel sure, a birthday present to many among his admirers.

That is my first qualification for appearing in the matter, but I have a second and more important one. Having for the last three years been engaged on Wodehouse's biography, I have read not merely the large part of his vast number of published works but also a great deal that has been written about him. I am, therefore, in a position to say that, although this is not exactly a critical piece, such as Hilaire Belloc's introduction to *Weekend Wodehouse* and Evelyn Waugh's much-quoted broadcast, it is in a different and subtle way an excellent appreciation of him.

He was not an author it was possible to parody. Many people have tried, but, although characters such as Jeeves and Bertie Wooster have individual characteristics so pronounced that it is easy to reproduce their speech and attitudes, no one that I have read has succeeded in anything better than a leaden imitation. The tricks are there, the dialogue is apt, but the spirit has escaped. Drs Morris and Macintyre are not attempting a parody of Wodehouse, and, if theirs is a parody at all, it is of work of a different kind. Yet, by the inspired gravity of tone and the talented use of quotation, they have succeeded in capturing the essence. In their pages Wodehouse lives again.

This is a work of exemplary scholarship, and, although the scholarship is itself part of the joke, it is nevertheless a lesson to the rest of us. These essays might be said to owe something to Monsignor Ronald Knox (another Oxford character) but, where such things as *Studies in the Literature of Sherlock Holmes* and *The Authorship of 'In Memoriam'* today seem ponderous, the authors of this book have the lightest touch; where the jokes in the earlier studies are only mildly funny, in these they are hilarious; and, best of all, where Knox does not entirely avoid the slightly superior tone of donnish writing of that date, the true affection these authors have for their subject is what makes this book so delightful.

I wish the Master himself might have read it. When the University of Oxford honoured him with a Doctorate of Letters, many of his vast reading public felt bewildered. They found it difficult to understand how anything which appealed so much to them could also appeal to Oxford (there remains some disbelief on this score). I hazard the guess that no one was more surprised than Wodehouse himself. He was read by Asquith when he was defeated and by Ronald Knox when he was dying; by M.R. James (of the other University) and myriads of devotees in every generation for pleasure. Yet, although he was so marvellously inspired, he felt that his proper place was among those people who write for money and to entertain the general public. He accepted the tributes paid to him with dignity but he found it difficult to understand them. I am sure he would have said that this book was full of *espièglerie* (see page 28). And he would have been right, because it is a highly successful *jeu d'esprit* (not part of Bertie Wooster's French vocabulary), while I have no hesitation in saying that the essay entitled *Bertie at Oxford* is a *tour de force* (again not part of Bertie's vocabulary) of the kind for which Wodehouse himself is famous.

All in all, a splendid private joke in which the public are lucky to participate. As long as Wodehouse is read, this book will surely continue to give pleasure.

FRANCES DONALDSON

PART 1.

BERTIE WOOSTER AND JEEVES

How old
was Bertie?

At first sight he never seems to grow any older throughout the Saga; perhaps it would be truer to say that, like Peter Pan, he never seems to grow up. Yet on closer inspection there are some indications that he does grow older. He acquires what he calls 'a vocabulary of sorts' from Jeeves. His facility for quotation certainly improves. He usually (but not invariably) gives Jeeves the credit for his knowledge of Shakespeare and the poets. On the other hand, he attributes his knowledge of the Bible entirely to the fact that he won a prize for Scripture Knowledge when at his prep. school. The surprising thing is that his memory of his schooldays improves significantly as the Saga progresses. There are also faint indications that he gets older physically as well as mentally. Thus, in 'The Great Sermon Handicap',[1] an early short story, he embarks on a twenty-mile bicycle ride without the slightest hesitation or (apparently) any ill effects. But in *Right Ho, Jeeves*,[2] a much later long story, he is appalled at the prospect of an eighteen-mile ride (admittedly this one is in the dark and without a lamp), protests that he hasn't ridden a bicycle for years, and returns with physical anguish in his backside, calves and ankles.

Before we can examine more closely this question of Bertie's age, we must first determine what span of time is covered by the stories. The evidence is as follows:

(i) Bertie was in America for over a year, unable to return to England because he believed that Aunt Agatha was sharpening her hatchet.[3]

(ii) Aunt Dahlia ran *Milady's Boudoir* for four years before it was 'sold to a mug up Liverpool way' called Lemuel Gengulphus Trotter.[4] There is, however, no evidence as to how long she had been running the paper when the Saga begins.

(iii) The first time Bertie mentions his Uncle Henry, he calls him 'my late Uncle Henry'.[5] In a much later story, he says that his Uncle Henry 'passed away three years ago'.[6]

(iv) Aunt Agatha's first husband was alive in two of the early short stories.[7] After his death she remained a widow 'for many years', and then married her second husband eighteen months before one of the later long stories begins.[8]

(v) Four of Bertie's Christmases are specifically accounted for: one at Twing, when Bingo Little presented a new and original review at the village hall, and got the bird from the audience because of the machinations of the wicked Steggles;[9] one at Skeldings, when Bobbie Wickham persuaded him to puncture Tuppy Glossop's hot-water bottle with a darning needle attached to a stick, but Tuppy changed rooms with his uncle Sir Roderick Glossop;[10] one at Bleaching Court, when young Tuppy suffered his ordeal in the rugby match between the two Hampshire villages;[11] and one at Brinkley Court, when Sir Roderick Glossop was prevailed upon to play Santa Claus at the children's party.[12] There is also the Christmas which Bertie must have spent in America, making five in all.

We shall do well to discount the inconclusive evidence of *Milady's Boudoir* and the conflicting evidence of Uncle Henry and Aunt Agatha, and concentrate our attention on the evidence of the five Christmases. This proves that the Saga spanned at least five years. One is reluctant to concede that it lasted any longer, partly because the indications that Bertie ever got any older are not very convincing, but mainly because the recurring regular characters never seem to do so – men like Bingo Little and Tuppy Glossop, girls like Honoria Glossop and Bobbie Wickham, even boys like young Thos. and Edwin, the Boy Scout (Jeeves is omitted, because he is clearly immortal). Young Thos., for instance, was aged fourteen in the second story in which he appears,[13] but is still at his prep. school in a much later story.[14] Edwin, the Boy Scout, perpetrates even more juvenile and ghastly horrors in a very late story[15] than he does in the very first story of all.[16]

How old was Bertie at the time of the stories? The evidence is as follows:

(i) In the very first story of all, when Bertie engages Jeeves and has not yet come into control of his money, he says that when Lord Worplesdon came after him with a hunting-crop for smoking one of his special cigars, he (Bertie) was 'a stripling of fifteen',[17] and that this happened 'nine years before'.[18] This would make Bertie twenty-four at the start of the Saga.

(ii) The twins Claude and Eustace were kids at school with Bertie in his last summer term[19] and were about four years younger than he was.[20] When they were sent down from Oxford for squirting soda-water at the Senior Tutor of their College, they must have been in either their first or their second year, because the Senior Tutor 'happened to be standing just outside our window'[21] – i.e. in College. Claude and Eustace must have needed a year or two at a crammer's after leaving Eton, in order to comply with the, admittedly not very exacting, admissions standards of the University of Oxford in the 1920s. (In one story, they are described as 'reading for some exam or other with the vicar'.[22]) That would make them about twenty-one, and Bertie about twenty-five.

(iii) Bingo Little says (and Bertie agrees) that they had been pals for fifteen years.[23] Bertie says that he and Bingo were born in the same village within a couple of days of one another, and went to kindergarten, Eton and Oxford together.[24] If we substitute 'prep. school' for 'kindergarten' and assume that the friendship began when they went there, presumably at the age of ten, that would make them both twenty-five.

(iv) Bertie's friend, Oliver Sipperley, was 'in his twenty-fifth year',[25] i.e. aged twenty-four. Oliver was a fellow-student of Gussie Fink-Nottle at the university.[26] (This university was probably Cambridge, for we are not told that either Oliver or Gussie was at Oxford with Bertie.) Gussie and Bertie were at prep. school and Eton together.[27] So they must all three have been contemporaries, though one has the impression that Bertie was the eldest.

(v) In a very late story, Bertie says that he had not seen the Reverend Aubrey Upjohn, the headmaster of his prep. school, for fifteen years.[28] If he went to Eton when he was thirteen or fourteen, this would make him twenty-eight or twenty-nine.

We conclude that Bertie was twenty-four at the time of the first story, when Uncle Willoughby was his trustee; that he acquired full control of his money at the age of twenty-five; and that he was between twenty-five and twenty-nine during the rest of the stories. Other commentators, however, maintain that his age remained static at about twenty-four[29] or twenty-five[30] throughout the Saga; but they do not examine the evidence.

2. WHO WAS TOM TRAVERS?

Bertie Wooster (Bertram Wilberforce Wooster,[1] to give him his full name) had a sister, Mrs Scholfield, who lived for a time in India and had three young daughters.[2] Bertie wanted to give up his London flat, take a house, and have them all to live with him. It was to frustrate this plan that Jeeves contrived to have Bertie make that memorable speech to the girls of Miss Tomlinson's school near Brighton. Mrs Scholfield is not mentioned again anywhere in the Saga, nor does Bertie ever mention any other sister or any brother; indeed, in one passage[3] he denies that he has any sisters. Mrs Scholfield evidently died young.

To make up for his lack of siblings, Bertie had an impressive array of uncles and aunts, of whom he mentions no less than fourteen. (It is well known that Wodehouse's fixation with aunts and uncles stems from the fact that when he was at school in England his parents lived in Hong Kong, where his father was a judge, and so during the holidays he was, to use his own expression, 'passed from aunt to aunt.'[4]) Here is a list of Bertie's uncles and aunts:

(i) *Uncle Cuthbert*. He had an expensive thirst, never backed a horse which did not develop housemaid's knee in the middle of the race, and had a bank-breaking system which caused the Monte Carlo administration to hang out the bunting and ring the joy-bells whenever he was sighted in the offing. Bertie was fond of him, but he died many years before the Saga begins. Bertie says that he had been the head of the family; presumably he was the eldest Wooster brother.[5]

(ii) *Aunt Julia*. The wife of Uncle Cuthbert. She was at one time a vaudeville artist and a good one, but after years of Aunt Agatha's society was indistinguishable from a dyed-in-the-wool aristocrat.[6] They had an only son, Gussie (not to be confused with Bertie's friend Gussie Fink-Nottle, the newt-fancier), who went to America and fell in love with a girl on the vaudeville stage. Aunt Agatha sent Bertie to America to disentangle Gussie from the clutches of this girl. But Bertie (who did not consult Jeeves) got the whole thing so mixed up that by the time he had finished his operations, Gussie not only married the girl but went on the stage himself and was doing well.[7] Aunt Julia married the girl's father, who turned out to be an old flame of her youth, and is heard of no more.

(iii) *Uncle Willoughby*. He was a 'white-haired old man' and either a baronet or a knight, for Jeeves calls him 'Sir Willoughby'.[8] He lived at Easeby in Shropshire and was writing his memoirs, which (surprisingly) included a 'dreadful story' about his neighbour, Lord Emsworth, in the days of his youth.[9] Bertie was at one time 'more or less dependent on Uncle Willoughby':[10] presumably he was Bertie's trustee.

(iv) *Aunt Agatha*. She was five feet nine inches tall, 'topped with a beaky nose, an eagle eye and a lot of grey hair'. Jeeves thought she was 'a forceful personality'. There was certainly no love lost between her and Bertie, who was scared stiff of her. She could, and frequently did, tick him off with surprising venom. He called her (but not of course to her face) 'the Pest of Pont Street, the human snapping turtle', 'the Family Curse', 'a werewolf', 'that great scourge of modern times'. He said that she wore barbed wire next the skin, ate broken bottles, killed rats with her teeth, and was known to devour her young and conduct human sacrifices at the time of the full moon.[11]

When she was young she was engaged to Lord Worplesdon, but broke it off on reading in the evening paper that he had been thrown out of a Covent Garden ball and taken to Vine Street Police Station in the company of a girl called Tottie.[12] She later married a stockbroker called Spenser Gregson. They had a town house in Pont Street and a country house at Woolam Chersey in Hertfordshire.[13] They had a son called Thomas ('young Thos.'), aged fourteen,[14] who, in Bertie's opinion, was 'notoriously a tough egg and a fiend in human shape'.[15] Spenser Gregson died[16] and, after remaining a widow for many years, Aunt Agatha returned to her first love and married Lord Worplesdon.[17] They lived at Bumpleigh Hall, Steeple Bumpleigh, Hampshire.[18]

(v) *Uncle Spenser*. Aunt Agatha's first husband. He was 'a battered little chappie on the Stock Exchange' who 'cleaned up to an amazing extent in Sumatra Rubber', and was thus able to buy that 'impressive' country house at Woolam Chersey.[19] He does not appear personally in any of the stories.

(vi) *Uncle Percy*, Lord Worplesdon, Aunt Agatha's second husband. He had a bristling moustache and the manners of a bear aroused while hibernating.[20] Bertie considered him 'a tough old egg with apparently not a spark of humanity in him, who had once held the metropolitan record for being chucked out of Covent Garden balls'.[21] He was a shipping magnate, the owner of the Pink Funnel Line.[22] He was more than a little eccentric.[23] Apparently he retained a sylph-like figure till well past middle age, because he could change clothes with Bertie[24] and no questions asked, not even by his wife Aunt Agatha, of whom he was scared stiff.[25]

Lord Worplesdon had been married before he married Aunt Agatha. By his previous marriage he had issue one daughter, Lady Florence Craye, who was engaged to be married to Bertie no less than four times[26] (once on his proposal, and three times on hers), and one son, Edwin the Boy Scout, aged fourteen, a ferret-faced kid whom Bertie had disliked from birth.[27] Lord Worplesdon had wanted to kick Edwin for years, but never had the nerve.[28]

(vii) *Uncle George*, later Lord Yaxley. He was a bachelor and a clubman for most of his life, 'a festive old bird who had made a habit for years of doing himself a dashed sight too well'.[29] Even Jeeves believed that 'if there was a defect in his lordship's mode of life, it was that he was a little unduly attached to the pleasures of the table –' ('Ate like a pig, you mean?').[30] As a result of his mode of life, Uncle George was frequently ordered to take the cure at Harrogate, and often insisted on Bertie accompanying him. Bertie did not like his Uncle George, who 'oppressed me sorely in my childhood'.[31] His favourite topic of conversation was the lining of his stomach.

There is some mystery about Uncle George's peerage. Evidently it was not conferred on him for public or political services, for he was idle and self-indulgent; besides, he 'came into the title',[32] which implies inheritance, not a new creation. Nor did he inherit it from his father, since if he did, his brothers and sisters would have been at least Hons; and if it had been an earldom, Aunt Agatha would have been Lady Agatha Gregson, and Aunt Dahlia, Lady Dahlia Travers. Moreover, in a very early story, Aunt Agatha says that there was no title in the family.[33] He must, therefore, have inherited it from some collateral relative. Why did he inherit it, and not Gussie (the son of Bertie's Uncle Cuthbert) or Uncle Willoughby? The answer must be that they died before Uncle George came into the title. Uncle George married late in life an old flame of his youth called Maudie Wilberforce, who had been a barmaid at the Criterion many years before, when Bertie was very young.[34] Presumably she was past the age of childbearing: and, consequently, Uncle George had no heir apparent. Who then was his heir presumptive? He must have been either Bertie or the elder of the two twins Claude and Eustace, depending on who was the elder, Bertie's father or his Uncle Henry.[35]

(viii) *Uncle Henry*. Bertie describes him as his 'late' Uncle Henry and says that he was 'by way of being the blot on the Wooster escutcheon. An extremely decent chappie personally, and one who had always endeared himself to me by tipping me with considerable lavishness when I was at school; but there's no doubt he did at times do some rather rummy things, notably keeping eleven pet rabbits in his bedroom; and I suppose a purist might have considered him more or less off his onion'. He wound up his career, happy to the last and completely surrounded by rabbits, in some sort of home. Aunt Agatha, on the other hand, jealous as always of the family name, insisted that he was nothing more than 'eccentric'.[36] It was this Uncle Henry who told Bertie, when he first came to London, that you could make a lot of money by betting that if you stood outside Romano's in the Strand you could see the clock on the wall of the Law Courts in Fleet Street – a story which formed the main theme of Bertie's stirring address to the girls of Miss Tomlinson's school.[37]

(ix) *Aunt Emily*. The wife of Uncle Henry. They had three sons, the twins Claude and Eustace,[38] who were sent down from Oxford for squirting soda-water at the Senior Tutor of their College (it takes more than that to get sent down from Oxford now) and were bundled off to South Africa by Aunt Agatha, despite their mother's no doubt tearful protestations:[39] and a much younger boy, Harold, who was aged six in the only story in which he is mentioned.

(x) *Uncle James*. When Bertie arrived with a birthday present for Harold which had set him back a mere elevenpence hapenny, he found Harold sitting in the midst of a mass of gifts so luxurious and costly that he hadn't the heart to contribute a present which had cost so little. 'So with rare presence of mind – for we Woosters can think quick on occasion – I wrenched my Uncle James's card off a toy aeroplane and substituted my own.'[40]

(xi) *Uncle Clive*. He lived in Worcestershire, and had Claude and Eustace to stay with him for two weeks after they had been sent down from Oxford.[41]

(xii) *Uncle Percy*. He is an even more shadowy figure. We are merely told that Bertie once 'was driven out of a thoroughly festive night club because the head waiter reminded me of my Uncle Percy';[42] and that, like so many of Bertie's friends and relations, Uncle Percy thought that he was a chump.[43] Both these allusions occur in early short stories, so this Uncle Percy cannot be the same as the Uncle Percy who married Aunt Agatha, because throughout the short stories she is called Mrs Spenser Gregson: she did not marry Lord Worplesdon until after the events narrated in *The Code of the Woosters*[44] and before those narrated in *Joy in the Morning*[45] and *The Mating Season*.[46]

(xiii) *Aunt Dahlia*. She was 'a large genial soul', 'a real good sort and a chirpy sportsman', with a brick-red face and a carrying voice due to having spent most of her youth hunting with the Quorn and Pytchley.[47] ('Has it ever occurred to you, Jeeves, that if all other sources of income failed, she could make a good living calling the cattle home across the Sands of Dee?'). Bertie says she was the only decent aunt he had.[48] She married Thomas Portarlington Travers *en secondes noces*[49] the year Bluebottle won the Cambridgeshire.[50] They had a town house in Charles Street, near Berkeley Square,[51] and a country house called Brinkley Court near Market Snodsbury in Worcestershire.[52] Nothing is known of Aunt Dahlia's first husband; he is not mentioned anywhere in the Saga and must have died when Bertie was quite young, or perhaps before Bertie was born. Aunt Dahlia had a daughter called Angela, of whom Bertie was fond, in a cousinly sort of way.[53] Angela was engaged to Tuppy Glossop and the engagement lasted at least two years.[54] Aunt Dahlia approved of the match; (she was extremely cross when it was three times temporarily broken off[55]), so Angela can hardly have been less than twenty when the engagement began. Aunt Dahlia also had a son called Bonzo, aged thirteen, who, in his mother's opinion, was and always had been a pest, but whom Bertie didn't mind.[56] We are not told in so many words that Angela and Bonzo were the children of Tom Travers as well as of Aunt Dahlia. Bonzo probably was, because Jeeves calls him 'Master Travers'; but Angela's case is much more debatable. She once called Tom 'father';[57] but this is far from conclusive, since a girl could easily call her step-father 'father', especially if her own father died many years ago. Moreover, Florence Craye once calls her step-mother (Aunt Agatha) 'mother', much to Bertie's astonishment.[58]

(xiv) *Uncle Tom*. Aunt Dahlia's second husband. He was a man with greyish hair and a face like a walnut.[59] He 'made a colossal pile of money out in the East, but in doing so put his digestion on the blink. This has made him a tricky proposition to handle. Many a time I've lunched with him and found him perfectly chirpy up to the fish, only to have him turn blue on me well before the cheese. . . . On these occasions he always seems to think he's on the brink of ruin and wants to start to economise.'[60] He once talked for days about 'ruin and the sinister trend of socialistic legislation and what will become of us all' – merely because he received a demand from the income tax people for an additional £58 1s 3d.[61] He collected old silver,[62] had a morbid dread of burglars[63] and of fire[64] and strongly objected to the presence of guests at Brinkley Court.[65] Marital relations between him and Aunt Dahlia seem to have ceased at the time of the Saga – at any rate, they occupied separate rooms.[66]

To complete the tale of Bertie's relations, we know that he had two more cousins besides the seven already mentioned (Gussie, Claude, Eustace, Harold, young Thos., Angela and Bonzo). One was a Theosophist[67] – we know nothing else about him, not even his name. The other was Aunt Dahlia's cousin Percy who, if Aunt Dahlia was a blood relation, must have been

Bertie's cousin once removed, though not necessarily a Wooster. He was a patient at Sir Roderick Glossop's clinic at Chuffnell Regis, because he believed that he was being followed about by little men with black beards.[68] It is quite possible that this cousin Percy is the same as the mysterious Uncle Percy (xii) previously mentioned, and that Bertie called him 'Uncle' out of courtesy, since he belonged to an older generation. Bertie also mentions an unnamed uncle, 'aged 76, who, under the influence of old crusted port, would climb trees'.[69] This, one feels, is most likely to have been Uncle Willoughby ('a white-haired old man') or possibly Uncle George or Cousin Percy, both of whom thought that alcohol was a food.[70]

It is quite certain that Bertie was an orphan, and probable that his parents died when he was quite young, before he was ten. He always refers to his 'late' father.[71] He only twice mentions his mother, once to say that when he was a child she thought him intelligent,[72] and once that when he was seven she thought he recited nicely.[73] And 'when he was a kid' he spent his holidays at Brinkley Court.[74]

The words 'uncle' and 'aunt' are unfortunately ambiguous: they could mean (a) the brother or sister of one's father, or (b) the brother or sister of one's mother, or (c) the wife or husband of (a) or (b). To which of these categories did Bertie's uncles and aunts belong? We start with the certainty that Aunt Agatha was the sister of Bertie's late father. For we are told quite distinctly that she was a Miss Wooster before she married Spenser Gregson.[75]

It is also clear that Uncle Cuthbert was a Wooster, for Bertie says that he had been the head of the family, and that Cuthbert's wife Julia was Aunt Agatha's sister-in-law.[76] It is true that their surname was not Wooster but Mannering-Phipps: but commentators have offered various ingenious explanations for this curious discrepancy.[77]

Uncle George was also probably a Wooster, even though Jeeves once calls him 'Mr George Travers'.[78] (The slip was corrected when that story was republished in the Omnibus edition.[79]) For if he had merely been a relation by marriage and not her brother, Aunt Agatha would not have been prepared to spend so much money in disentangling him from Maudie, the barmaid at the Criterion,[80] and years later from her niece Rhoda Platt, a waitress at Uncle George's club.[81] Besides, Maudie knew him as George ('Piggie') Wooster before he came into the title.[82]

It is also probable that Uncle Henry was a Wooster, for otherwise Aunt Agatha would not have been so solicitous in defending him from Bertie's charge that he was 'more or less off his onion' and maintaining that he was merely eccentric,[83] or so officious in bundling Claude and Eustace off to South Africa against their mother's wishes after their disgrace at Oxford.[84] True, she might have done either of these things if Emily, Henry's wife, had been her sister. But Bertie states distinctly that 'my late Uncle Henry was by way of being the blot on the *Wooster* escutcheon',[85] and surely that is conclusive.

Uncle Clive was also probably a Wooster, since otherwise he would not have offered Claude and Eustace hospitality for a fortnight after their disgrace at Oxford.[86] True, he might have done so if he had been Emily's brother, but in that case he would not have been Bertie's uncle.

Uncle James was probably a Wooster, since one does not usually give expensive birthday presents to the nephew of one's brother-in-law.

Uncle Willoughby was more probably a Wooster than not (one can put it no higher), because Bertie's money is more likely to have been derived from his father than from his mother, and his father is more likely to have appointed his brother than his brother-in-law to be Bertie's trustee.

We have now provided Bertie's father with one sister (Agatha) and six brothers (Cuthbert, Willoughby, George, Henry, Clive and James). It begins to look as though Bertie's mother must have been an only child. Only three characters remain to be disposed of: Uncle Percy, Aunt Dahlia and Uncle Tom. Uncle Percy is too colourless a character to place in any category; there is no evidence about him at all. As to Aunt Dahlia and Uncle Tom, there is no lack of evidence, but at first sight it is conflicting. Here is the crucial passage in which Aunt Dahlia is first introduced; it is one of the most difficult in the whole Saga to interpret: 'She married my Uncle Thomas – between ourselves a bit of a squirt – the year Bluebottle won the Cambridgeshire; and they hadn't got half way down the aisle before I was saying to myself, "That woman is much too good for the old bird".[87]

The natural interpretation of this passage is that Tom Travers had always been Bertie's uncle, and so must have been his mother's brother; and that Bertie hadn't met Aunt Dahlia before the wedding, and so she must have been an aunt by marriage. But this interpretation will not do; first, because at the time of the wedding Bertie must have been far too young to realise that Aunt Dahlia was 'much too good for the old bird'; and secondly, because it is flatly contradicted by evidence from later stories which proves conclusively that Aunt Dahlia was a blood relation and Uncle Tom an uncle by marriage.

How old was Bertie at the time of the wedding? He could not have been more than eleven, and may have been much younger. The evidence is as follows:

(i) Bertie, as we have seen,[88] was aged twenty-five to twenty-nine in most of the stories. His cousin Angela, Aunt Dahlia's daughter, cannot have been less than twenty at the beginning of her engagement to Tuppy Glossop, i.e. about five or six years younger than Bertie. That would make Bertie only four or five at the time of the wedding, if Angela was Uncle Tom's daughter; but, as we have seen, there is insufficient evidence to prove this, though reputable commentators are convinced that she was.[89]

(ii) Bonzo was probably the son of Uncle Tom as well as of Aunt Dahlia. He was thirteen in the only story in which he makes a personal appearance, i.e. about twelve years younger than Bertie. So Bertie cannot have been more than eleven at the time of the wedding.

(iii) Bertie says that Uncle Tom had been collecting old silver 'since I was so high',[90] and that when he was at his prep. school Uncle Tom 'often sent me postal orders for as much as ten bob'.[91] So, if Uncle Tom was a relation by marriage, the wedding must have taken place well before Bertie went to Eton.

It follows that the passage introducing Aunt Dahlia which was quoted above cannot be taken literally and that we must look for some other explanation of her relationship to Bertie. Here is a summary of the evidence:

(i) Aunt Dahlia says that she frequently dandled Bertie on her knee as a baby[92] and that, on one occasion when she was left alone with him in his cradle, he nearly swallowed his rubber comforter and started turning purple – she removed it and saved his life.[93] So Aunt Dahlia must have known him long before the wedding.

(ii) Bertie says that 'the years rolled away from her and Aunt Dahlia was once more the Dahlia Wooster of the old yoicks and tantivy days.'[94]

(iii) There are several passages in which Bertie says that Aunt Dahlia married 'old Tom Travers' (not 'my Uncle Tom').[95]

(iv) Bertie often says specifically that Aunt Dahlia was 'my late father's sister';[96] and Aunt Dahlia says that Bertie was her brother's son.[97]

(v) Bertie comments on the curious fact that two such dissimilar personalities as Aunt Dahlia and Aunt Agatha should have been sisters.[98]

It is therefore clear that, at any rate in the later stories, Aunt Dahlia was a Wooster, the sister of Bertie's late father. However, it is difficult to disagree with one commentator (Usborne) who is convinced that she was originally intended to be an aunt by marriage.[99]

It is easy to dispose of the possibility that Uncle Tom was Bertie's mother's brother. First, he often calls him 'my uncle by marriage'.[100] Secondly, Bertie says that Sir Reginald Witherspoon, Bart., who was his host one Christmas, 'married Aunt Dahlia's husband's younger sister Katherine'.[101] This would be a strange way of describing Katherine if she had been a maternal aunt.[102]

There are certain discrepancies in what we are told about Tom Travers which remain to be considered. First, he wouldn't live in the country;[103] yet he bought Brinkley Court soon after he was married.[104] Secondly, he couldn't stick the south of France at any price;[105] yet he went there to get away from guests at Brinkley Court,[106] and on another occasion even went for a cruise to the Mediterranean in his yacht. They sailed from Southampton, and the cruise was postponed for a month owing to the illness of Anatole, his French chef.[107] One wonders whether they went through the French canals, or via Gibraltar. The latter seems more likely, since a vessel large enough to contain Anatole and his impedimenta must have been too large to pass through the canals.

Bertie was prepared to tolerate Tom Travers, presumably for Aunt Dahlia's sake. On one occasion he journeyed from Totleigh Towers in Gloucestershire to Brinkley Court in Worcestershire in order to have lunch with Uncle Tom in Aunt Dahlia's absence, which he considered preferable to attending a school treat.[108] But there can be no doubt that Bertie was right in his view that she was much too good for the old bird: though whether he really thought so at their wedding is open to serious doubt.

Tom Travers: a case for the defence
By A. D. Macintyre

The critic Morris concludes his analysis of the Tom Travers problem by agreeing with Bertie's view that Aunt Dahlia was 'much too good for the old bird'. But much of the evidence supports a more favourable estimate of Uncle Tom. First, there can be no doubt that Aunt Dahlia, herself a formidable personality, was fond of her husband, respected him and feared his wrath. They were 'a fond and united couple'.[109] Yet Uncle Tom's wrath was never actually exercised – a point worth emphasising and a clear sign of his essential kindness and forbearance towards his wife. Instead, we find him paying out considerable sums towards the cost of *Milady's Boudoir*, the weekly paper run at a loss by Aunt Dahlia. Footing these bills was, according to Bertie, 'a source of considerable spiritual agony' to Uncle Tom: 'He has the stuff in sackfuls, but he hates to part.'[110] Before accepting this accusation of meanness, several points must be weighed. First, Bertie's financial ethic was poles apart from his uncle's. How could he begin to understand the latter's not unreasonable fears about the apparently never-ending demands of *Milady's Boudoir*? Second, Bertie was proud of the 'piece as we writers call it', entitled 'What the Well Dressed Man Is Wearing' which he contributed to the paper. He had a personal interest in the fate of the paper ('a soft spot' in his heart always existed for it: 'we old journalists do have these feelings'[111]), quite apart from the fact that it was run by his beloved aunt, and these points must be borne in mind in interpreting his sharp verdict on the man on whom the paper depended. For, despite all his reservations, well and wittily summed up in his habit of alluding to the paper as 'Madame's Nightshirt',[112] Uncle Tom always paid up. This was striking altruism in a man with strongly-held views on money (and on taxation) and with his own interests as a knowledgeable and determined collector of old silver. Bertie entirely failed to sympathise with his uncle's enthusiasm as a collector who rejoiced in a good piece and who liked to talk to Bertie about his collection at some length.

One further important point must be remembered in assessing Bertie's judgment of his uncle. Aunt Dahlia was loved by Bertie, and in most matters one respects his judgment. But in Uncle Tom's case, it was seriously warped by feelings of Wooster family solidarity, the well-known Wooster pride. Aunt Dahlia differed in many respects from her sister Agatha, but undoubtedly shared with her qualities of toughness and ruthlessness. She cannot have been entirely easy to live with. Not to put too fine a point on it, she had strong elements of the criminal in her, and Al Capone could profitably have taken her correspondence course. Unlike Aunt Agatha, she was quite ready to resort to violence, and coshed Roderick Spode as to the manner born: 'I took a nice easy half-swing and let go with lots of follow-through, and he fell to earth he knew not where'.[113] She readily commissioned theft, and was prepared in an emergency to carry out theft herself. It comes as no surprise to learn that when young she had blackmailed her governess whom she had seen being kissed by her brother George.[114] Her business ethics ('salting the mine' to persuade L. G. Trotter of the viability of *Milady's Boudoir*) left much to be desired.[115] We can only guess at why she and Uncle Tom occupied separate rooms, but Aunt Dahlia's carrying voice, product of her early years with the Quorn and Pytchley, may have been a factor on his side of the matter. Any man who could live with her earns one's respect, amounting to awe, mingled with some sympathy. Even Bertie, much as he loved her, was forced to comment severely on the laxity of her moral code.[116]

Uncle Tom's occasionally inconsistent behaviour, to which the critic Morris alludes, demonstrated a reasonable flexibility in situations which often called for that quality. In the course of life with Aunt Dahlia, he had sound reasons for fearing burglars and fire. He certainly had excellent grounds for disliking some of the guests at Brinkley Court, such as Ma Trotter and Percy Gorringe, quite apart from the fact that he had not invited them. If we bear in mind his difficulties with his digestion, which could play him up not only if he succumbed to lobsters and cucumber but even at the mere sight of Percy Gorringe's pushing away Anatole's food untasted, he will readily be forgiven a certain crustiness.[117] He was, Bertie said, capable of being 'perfectly chirpy'. We can safely conclude that he was a remarkably tolerant husband (although by no means a toad beneath his wife's harrow), a cultivated man and, from a point of view not unusual among merchant princes, a realist – though possibly also something of a bore – in the matter of 'the sinister trend of socialistic legislation'. He liked cigars, loved his garden and suffered from insomnia (the latter surely contributing its bit to his crustiness).[118] He had served in the East Worcestershire Volunteers and was a Freemason. In one important respect, *he* was 'too good' for Aunt Dahlia: he had no criminal tendencies. Bertie's confidential view of him – 'between ourselves a bit of a squirt' – had a distinct ring of shamefacedness about it. And well might Bertie have felt ashamed. For his uncle, besides sending five and ten bobs regularly to him at school (not inconsiderable sums to a preparatory-school boy), had provided a home in the school holidays for the orphaned Bertie. He was also the employer of the great Anatole, for whose cooking Bertie had such a high and deserved regard. We should judge a man by his cook as well as by his valet. Bertie's agreement to keep Uncle Tom company in Aunt Dahlia's absence indicated not merely his readiness to do his aunt a good turn but also that he had come to modify a severe verdict on his uncle formed at so early an age and in circumstances (during the latter's wedding) rarely conducive to sound judgment. 'A kindly old bimbo': this was Bertie's considered view of his uncle. With Bertie's cautious qualification that even kindly old bimbos can make themselves unpleasant when conditions are right, I think this should be our view also of Tom Travers. In short, as Bertie also said, he was 'a pleasant old bird'.[119]

A further suggestion. Was he partly Irish? It seems possible. Bertie, himself presumably English to the core, was astonished at his uncle's middle name of Portarlington, and reflected that 'there's some raw work pulled at the font from time to time'.[120] But if one of Uncle Tom's parents, perhaps his mother, since middle names often reflect a maternal connection, was descended from the Dawson-Damer family, Earls of Portarlington, the 'raw work' may be explained. There is another possibility. The little town of Portarlington, Co. Leix (formerly Queen's Co.), population 2,720 in 1962, owes its 'tall and dignified houses and the extensive orchards and gardens' to the industrious Huguenot settlers established there by General Ruvigny, Earl of Galway, during William III's reign.[121] It could be that Tom Travers – the name has a Huguenot ring to it – came from one of those families.

3. BERTIE AT OXFORD

I. WHICH WAS HIS COLLEGE?

Bertie says quite distinctly that Magdalen was his College,[1] so one would think there could be no argument about that. Yet some critics have doubted his statement,[2] merely on the strength of his friend Chuffy's remark (which they not only misquote but also attribute to Bertie) that once after a bump supper he 'insisted that he was a mermaid and wanted to dive into the College fountain and play the harp'.[3] The critic French wonders whether perhaps Bertie meant Christ Church, since 'one is always mixing up these colleges'; and concludes that 'there was a fountain in Bertie's Magdalen, because Wodehouse put one there'.[4] Of course, no Magdalen man of spirit can stick this sort of thing at any price. The explanation of the fountain is really very simple. For it is (or was) the custom at Oxford bump suppers to invite one representative from each of the bumped boats. We have only to imagine that the Christ Church boat bumped the Magdalen boat, and that Bertie was the Magdalen representative at the Christ Church bump supper, and the problem is solved. There is no evidence that Chuffy was at Magdalen; being a lord, he was much more likely to have been at Christ Church. And Bertie did row for a time at Oxford, even though his main athletic achievement was his racquets blue.[5] He tells us that in a weak moment, misled by his advisers, he tried to do a bit of rowing,[6] but gave it up because he discovered that dipping an oar in the water, giving it a shove, and hauling it out again was not only silly but also the deuce of a sweat.[7] There is, indeed, some evidence that he got into the Magdalen first eight. For when the magistrate at Vinton Street police court lunched with his nephew Stilton Cheesewright soon after fining Bertie £10 for obstructing a policeman in the execution of his duty, he noticed a group photograph in which Bertie appeared, and recognised his face.[8] This can hardly have been a freshman's or a Commem. Ball photograph, since the magistrate would surely not have recognised Bertie's face 'on leaving' amid the sea of others. It can only have been a rowing photograph, for Stilton never did anything else except row – he rowed four years for Oxford.[9] It must have been a photograph of the Magdalen first eight, since Stilton, being a blue, would not have rowed in Torpids.

The question of Bertie's College being thus satisfactorily settled, the next question is, what did he read?

II. What did he read?
By A. D. Macintyre

Bertie, although modest enough to accept the label 'chump' as applying to himself, said that Gussie Fink-Nottle 'had always stood by himself in the chump class': '... at our private school ... he had been known as "Fathead", and that was in competition with fellows like Bingo Little, Freddie Widgeon and myself'.[10] Yet Gussie, while showing on occasion that this reputation was deserved, revealed in *The Code of the Woosters* a decidedly unchumplike force of character in standing up to Roderick Spode, the amateur dictator. Furthermore, Gussie was dedicated to his research on the habits of newts, having doubtless acquired some qualification for the task at the university which he attended along with Oliver Sipperley. In Bertie's judgment of Gussie and his life's work – 'a strong newt complex ... this kink in Gussie's character'[11] – we have a graphic illustration long before C. P. Snow of the division of cultures, of the inability of the Arts man (which Bertie must have been) to understand the Scientist.

William, ninth Earl of Rowcester, was thought in the Drones Club to rank intellectually somewhere between Freddie Widgeon and Pongo Twistleton, i.e. pretty low. Some even thought his I.Q. inferior to that of Barmy Fotheringay Phipps.[12] Bertie's

confident placing of his friends in the matter of intellect indicated
that he thought others had powerful claims to be regarded as
greater chumps than himself. Sir Roderick Glossop, the eminent
nerve specialist, of course thought otherwise, at least in the
earlier phases of his relations with Bertie.

Bertie was an admirable pupil, particularly of Jeeves, always
enthusiastic and open-minded if not always accurate in his quo-
tations and in citing (or remembering) his authorities. He was
nearly always ready to take advice on important matters (e.g.
Nietzsche, rowing). In some ways he was too good a pupil, being
inclined to attribute all good things to his tutor – a habit of mind
possibly more widespread in his Oxford days than in ours. He
had a pretty sound and independently-formed knowledge of
Scripture – a point on which he often insisted: his grasp of the
essentials of the history of Mrs Lot was equalled only by his fear
that others might not be familiar with it.[13] Now Jeeves rarely
quoted from Scripture. He was able to remind Bertie who Jezebel
was, although only a jog was necessary – Bertie remembered at
once that she was eaten by dogs; and Jeeves acted as arbitrator
between Bertie and Bobbie Wickham on the question of whether
it was Balaam or Jonah who had the ass, coming down on the
side of Bertie (and Balaam).[14] But relatively few of Jeeves's good
things came from the Bible. If he had a blind spot, this was it.
Lack of sound early training in this respect probably contributed
to his ruthlessness. Jeeves was not meek. Bertie was, and he shall
inherit the earth.

Lacking firm evidence but going on the principle of excluding
the impossible in the search for the possible, I suggest that Bertie
may have read Theology at Magdalen, though I am unable to
say with what result. He shows no knowledge of any mathematical theorem or scientific law. He seems to have had little
Latin apart from what Jeeves put over to him, and less Greek.
He never reads the newspapers, so it is safe to assume that he did
not read Modern Greats (P.P.E.). Regretfully we must exclude
Law: entering a *nolle prosequi* was learnt from Jeeves, and
appearances in court as a defendant were Bertie's only other
connection with the law. The only history he frequently mentioned concerned the early Woosters at the time of the Norman
Conquest and in the Crusades, though there were passing

references to some old Puritan strain in the Wooster blood and to an ancestor ('Wellington always used to say he was the best spy he ever had') in the Peninsular War.[15] He did not know that Tolstoy was either a Russian or a novelist or dead; he thought Turgenev and Dostoevsky were 'a couple of Russian exiles', still alive, who 'did a bit of writing on the side'.[16] One might reasonably expect rather more from an Oxford-trained historian. We are left with Theology. We know that it was intellectually his longest suit, grounding in which was obtained at a time when his mother thought him intelligent. It is true that he nowhere gave us any guidance on the matter of his School at Oxford. But he might well have felt some reserve about airing the matter since, unlike his old Magdalen friend, Harold ('Stinker') Pinker, he did not see the light and take holy orders. (It is also quite possible that he did not get a degree.) In this connection, we should perhaps remember that Bertie bore the great Anglican and Evangelical name of Wilberforce. Samuel Wilberforce, the third son of the politician and abolitionist, William Wilberforce, was Bishop of Oxford 1845–69; and his nickname of 'Soapy Sam' might have been coined in the nineteenth-century equivalent of the Drones Club.

III. WHAT DID HE READ?
By J. H. C. Morris

The critic Macintyre points out, with obvious correctness, that Bertie shows no knowledge of any mathematical or scientific principle; and that he seems to have little Latin (apart from what Jeeves taught him) and less Greek. Macintyre briefly examines and rejects the possibilities that he read P.P.E., History or Law and concludes (somewhat rashly, it would seem) 'we are left with Theology'. However, the matter is not quite so simple; the evidence must be properly marshalled before any conclusion can safely be hazarded.

(i) *P.P.E.* Macintyre says that Bertie 'never reads the newspapers, so it is safe to assume that he did not read Modern Greats'. This is an amusing side-swipe at our Social Studies colleagues, but even if true it seems slender evidence for so sweeping a conclusion. And (with great respect) it is not true. Bertie once says that 'bar a weekly wrestle with the *Pink 'Un* and an occasional dip into the form book, I'm not much of a lad for reading';[17] but I think he must have been exaggerating. True, he never gives the financial pages a glance;[18] but he does read the sporting and engagement columns of *The Times*[19] and the *Morning Post*,[20] and even has a shot at *The Times*[21] and *Telegraph*[22] crossword puzzles. His preferred breakfast reading is the *Mirror* and the *Mail*,[23] and when staying with his friend Rockmeteller Todd in the wilds of Long Island, New York, he complains that you have to walk six miles for an evening paper.[24] Moreover, he once reads in the paper about 'those birds who are trying to split the atom, the nub being that they haven't the foggiest as to what will happen if they do. It may be all right. On the other hand, it may not be all right'[25] – which seems a very neat summary of what was once a complex scientific problem.

The main evidence that Bertie at least began to read P.P.E. at Oxford is his statement that 'they' tried to make him read Schopenhauer.[26] It does not sound as though 'their' efforts were very successful, and I do not think he progressed very far in his study of philosophy. He found *Types of Ethical Theory* very heavy going,[27] shied away from Nietzsche like a startled colt[28] and thought that Spinoza was a living author of whodunnits.[29] Add to this his complete ignorance of economics and politics (he has never heard of the Right Hon. A. B. Filmer, a Cabinet Minister,[30] or the would-be dictator Roderick Spode[31]), and I think we shall be safe in concluding that he did not read P.P.E.

(ii) *Law*. The critic Macintyre regretfully excludes Law on the ground that the only legal term Bertie ever uses (entering a *nolle prosequi*) he demonstrably learnt from Jeeves. This is true, but it is fair to point out that he does have a curious fixation with the minor crime of failing to abate a smoky chimney.[32] Can we deduce from this that he once wrote an essay on the distinction between public and private nuisance, or even one on the difference between tort and crime? Hardly. I do not think he read Law.

(iii) *History*. The critic Macintyre dismisses History on the ground that the only historical events with which Bertie seems familiar are the Norman Conquest[33] and the Crusades,[34] in each of which his ancestors played a not unworthy part. However, he also mentions his ancestors' prowess at the Battles of Crécy[35] and Agincourt;[36] nor is he a mere narrow medievalist, because he has also heard of that sunken road at Waterloo which disrupted the French cavalry charge.[37] But on the whole, with some doubts, I am inclined to agree with Macintyre's conclusion that 'one might reasonably expect rather more from an Oxford-trained historian'.

(iv) *Theology*. Macintyre concludes (though he admits that 'firm' evidence is lacking) that Bertie read Theology at Magdalen, on the grounds that (a) theology was intellectually his long suit, and (b) he bore the great Anglican and Evangelical name of Wilberforce. Let us examine these two statements.

(a) It is quite true that, particularly in the later stories, Bertie does parade his knowledge of the Bible and especially of the Old Testament. He knows that Mrs Lot was turned into a pillar of salt, and why; that there was writing on the wall at Belshazzar's feast (a gag which he thought was worked with mirrors); that Job had boils, and Nabob a vineyard; that manna descended from the skies on the children of Israel in the wilderness; that Daniel entered the lions' den, and Shadrach, Mesach and Abednego the burning fiery furnace; that Jonah had a whale, and Balaam an ass which was inclined to enter *nolle prosequis*, dig its feet in, and refuse to play ball; that Jezebel was eaten by dogs; and that the deaf adder stopped its ears and would not hear the voice of the charmer. He has heard of Hittites, Hivites and Jebusites; of the parable of the talents and of the prodigal son; and of Samson and Delilah, but not what they did to each other. He knows that Jael, the wife of Heber, dug spikes into the guest's coconut while he was asleep, but not the name of the guest, nor the tribe to which the host belonged. But all this magpie-like miscellany of knowledge can easily be attributed (as Bertie himself attributes it) to that Scripture Knowledge prize which he won at his prep. school. Surely it is prep. school stuff, reinforced perhaps by 'Divvers', not the stuff of which Honour Schools are made. There are no indications that Bertie knows anything of ecclesiastical history or doctrine, or even of the New Testament, except the names of a couple of parables. One might reasonably expect rather more from an Oxford-trained theologian.

(b) As for the curious argument that Bertie must have read Theology because his parents christened him Wilberforce eighteen years before he came up to Oxford, it is easily refuted. For Aunt Dahlia tells him that he was called Wilberforce because the day before his christening his father won a packet on an outsider of that name in the Grand National.[38] So his middle name was derived from equine sources, not evangelical ones.

Macintyre's theory that Bertie read Theology is thus one that cannot be accepted. It remains to examine two other Honour Schools which, though not mentioned by Macintyre, deserve to be considered.

(v) *English*. When he was at school, Bertie's English composition reports usually read 'Has little or no ability, but does his best'. In the course of years, he picked up a vocabulary of sorts from Jeeves.[39] He often boasts that he can tell a story lucidly and well. But he cannot recognise the most hackneyed quotation from Shakespeare or the poets, no matter how many times he has heard it before from Jeeves. He has not heard of Shelley,[40] Wordsworth[41] or Thomas Hardy,[42] though he has heard of Omar Khayyam, and can even recognise his poetry when he hears it read aloud.[43] He has some curious, and not easily reconcilable, ideas about Shakespeare. He thinks that Burns wrote *Hamlet*;[44] that Shakespeare wrote Kipling's poem about the female of the species;[45] that what Shakespeare wrote sounds well, but doesn't mean anything;[46] and that half the time Shakespeare just shoved down anything that came into his head.[47] Passages indicating that he thinks Jeeves wrote most of Shakespeare's better-known cracks are too numerous to mention here. No, I don't think anyone can seriously maintain that Bertie read English at Oxford.

(vi) *Modern Languages (French)*. Insufficient attention has been paid to the remarkable number of French words and phrases which Bertie not only knows, but knows how to spell and how to use in the proper context. These are scattered throughout the Saga, though most of them occur in *Right Ho, Jeeves*, which he wrote soon after his return from a two-month holiday at Cannes. Here is a list: abattoir - amende honorable

– amour propre – à quoi sort-il? – armoire – arrière pensée – au pied de la lettre – bien être – bijouterie – bonhomie – bouillon – boulevardier – camaraderie – chapeau – chez – conte – critique – débris – déja vu – de rigueur – diablerie – élan – embonpoint – en déshabillé – en masse – ennui – en route – en secondes noces – espièglerie – faute de mieux – femme fatale – flâneur – force majeure – frappé – frisson – gaffe – gants – gendarmerie – grande dame – hauteur – idée fixe – impasse – insouciance – j'accuse – je ne sais quoi – joie de vivre – j'y suis, j'y reste – macédoine – mal au foie – mélange – morale – morceau – motif – mot juste – moue – mousse – mousseline – noblesse oblige – objet d'art – perdu – personnel – petite – pique – preux chevalier – plat du jour – point d'appui – pot-pourri – pourparlers – précis – purée – raisonneur – régime – rôle – salle de bain – salon – sangfroid – sec – 'smoking' (meaning dinner jacket) – soigné – solitude à deux – tête à tête – timbre – tout ce qu'il y a de chic – tout comprendre c'est tout pardonner – tout ensemble – vis-à-vis – voilà tout.

Surely this list is most impressive. If Bertie's English vocabulary was as limited as he would have us believe, he must have been almost bilingual. It is true that he is not so strong on the literature side of the School: but he does know that Cyrano de Bergerac had a large nose.[48] I should hesitate to conclude from this that he read Modern Languages; but I think it far more likely that he read Modern Languages than Theology.

My own opinion, for what it is worth, is that he read the Groups of the Pass School. I just don't think he had the type of mind which one associates with an Honours man – the ability to handle several difficult subjects all at the same time, and to perceive the relation between them. There is a revealing passage in which he says that at Oxford he was content just to exist beautifully.[49] Is that not one of the hallmarks of the pass man? After all, we know that Warren's Magdalen was full of them. I visualise his Oxford career as follows: the vicar of Twing in Gloucestershire successfully coached him through Smalls[50] (i.e. Responsions) and probably 'Divvers' as well; he then read Pass Mods., which in those days was the recognised prelim. for several other Honour Schools besides Greats; he may have started his first summer term on the philosophy side of P.P.E., though personally I doubt it; if he did, he soon gave it up and switched to a Pass School.

IV. DID HE GET A DEGREE?

The final question is, did he get a degree? There is a scintilla of evidence that he did, provided one interprets it in one of three possible ways; and there is a great mass of evidence which suggests, though indirectly, that he did not.

The positive evidence is as follows. Bertie is surprised to hear that his friend Bingo Little has been staying at Ditteredge Hall in Hampshire, for his loathing for the country was well known. Bingo explains that because an absolute sitter came unstitched at Haydock Park, he has been forced to take a job tutoring Sir Roderick Glossop's son Oswald. Bertie is surprised: 'I couldn't seem to see young Bingo as a tutor. Though, of course, he did get a degree of sorts at Oxford, and I suppose you can always fool some of the people some of the time.'[51] Now, what did Bertie mean by those two cryptic words 'of course'? Three explanations suggest themselves:

(i) He may have thought that anyone who sat an examination for a degree at Oxford automatically got one. If so, he was of course quite wrong, and surely he must have known that he was wrong.

(ii) He may have meant to convey that no one in his or Bingo's set at Oxford, however chump-like, could ever fail to get a degree. If so, unless he was being unusually devious, he must have got a degree himself.

(iii) A third explanation, which I regard as the most likely, is that the words mean nothing at all: they are comparable with the meaningless 'Haws' with which, according to Mrs Woodham Smith, English cavalry officers used to interlard their conversation at the time of the Crimean War, or the equally meaningless 'You knows' with which the young interlard their conversation today.

The negative evidence is as follows. There are two intellectual achievements in his life about which Bertie boasts with monotonous regularity. One is the prize for Scripture Knowledge which he won at his prep. school. The other is the piece he contributed to *Milady's Boudoir* on 'What the Well-Dressed Man is Wearing'. Never once does he mention that he is a Bachelor of Arts (Oxon.). When Vanessa Cook tells him she doesn't suppose he has ever done anything worth-while in his life,[52] he does not tell her (as he might have told Madeline Bassett's friend Hilda Gudgeon, the solid girl) that he got a racquets blue. He knows that that would not have impressed a left-wing intellectual like Vanessa. Nor does he tell her that he is a B.A. Indeed, he does not tell her anything. 'I could have made her look pretty silly by revealing that I had won a Scripture Knowledge prize at my private school and contributed an article to *Milady's Boudoir* on "What the Well-Dressed Man is Wearing" ': but he decides to let it go. The conclusion seems inescapable: he left Oxford without a degree. I think he just failed; I do not think he was sent down. After all, the Senior Deans of Arts in Warren's time must have had to be pretty tolerant. And there is no vice in Bertie. He is meek and gentle; except when drunk, he knows how to behave; and what Senior Dean is going to send down a racquets blue just because he is mildly intoxicated at a bump supper?

4. BERTIE'S DRINKING HABITS

It was one of Aunt Dahlia's most cherished beliefs that Bertie never stopped drinking, even when he was asleep:

> She paused, and allowed her eye to roam thoughtfully over my perhaps somewhat corpse-like face.
>
> 'So you were out on the tiles last night, were you, my little chickadee? It's an extraordinary thing – every time I see you, you appear to be recovering from some debauch. Don't you ever stop drinking? How about when you are asleep?'
>
> I rebutted the slur.
>
> 'You wrong me, relative. Except at times of special revelry, I am exceedingly moderate in my potations. A brace of cocktails, a glass of wine at dinner and possibly a liqueur with the coffee – that is Bertram Wooster. But last night I gave a small bachelor binge for Gussie Fink-Nottle.'[1]

There are many other passages in the same vein.[2]

Yet the evidence tends to support Bertie's view that he was a moderate, or even an abstemious, drinker. 'Abstemious cove though I am as a general thing,' he says, 'there is one night in the year when, putting all other engagements aside, I am rather apt to let myself go a bit and renew my lost youth, as it were. The night to which I allude is ... Boat Race night.'[3] On one of these occasions, he persuaded his friend Oliver Sipperley to pinch a policeman's helmet when the policeman was inside it, for which he spent a night in a cell and was fined £5 next morning at Bosher Street Police Court by Sir Watkyn Bassett, Madeline's father.[4] On a much earlier occasion, during his second year at Oxford (well before the Saga begins), he had the presence of mind to tell the magistrates that his name was Eustace H. Plimsoll and that he lived at The Laburnums, Alleyn Road, West Dulwich.[5]

There are only four occasions in the whole Saga, covering a span of five years, when Bertie admits to having a hangover and to be in need of one of Jeeves's special pick-me-ups: but on each occasion one feels that there were extenuating circumstances. The first was when he had been staying in the country with his Uncle Willoughby, and his fiancée, Lady Florence Craye, had been making him read a book called *Types of Ethical Theory*, and Meadowes, his man, was sneaking his silk socks – 'a thing no bloke of spirit could stick at any price'.[6] So Bertie had to come to London to get a new man – and who shall blame him if he attended 'a rather cheery little supper'? The second occasion was the morning when Sir Watkyn Bassett fined him £5,[7] as already mentioned. The third was the morning after Pongo Twistleton's birthday party at the Drones,[8] on returning from which Bertie mistook the standard lamp for a burglar.[9] And the fourth was after his dinner party at the Drones to celebrate Gussie Fink-Nottle's engagement to Madeline Bassett.[10]

Even when he was up at Oxford, Bertie never seems to have got drunk except at bump suppers. On one of these occasions 'he insisted that he was a mermaid and wanted to dive into the College fountain and play the harp'.[11] On others, 'he used to take all his clothes off and ride round the quad on a bicycle, singing comic songs'.[12]

But in his later years, Bertie was a man of much more sober habits. He seldom entered a pub. He rarely had a drink in the morning, even at the Drones.[13] He disliked drinking alone, at any rate in public.[14] Jeeves had instructions to bring him his whisky and siphon every evening, and did so with a punctuality which Bertie sometimes found monotonous.[15] Two cocktails before dinner were generally his limit.[16] Even when he was nerving himself to set a booby trap for Oliver Sipperley's old headmaster, in the form of a pound and a half of flour balanced on top of an office door, Bertie's lunch drinks consisted merely of 'a couple of dry Martinis, half a bottle of nice light dry champagne, and a spot of brandy'.[17] And when Bertie attended that fancy dress dance at East Wibley Town Hall, he was perfectly sober, but his Uncle Percy (Lord Worplesdon) was extremely tight.[18]

It is true that Gussie Fink-Nottle once says that Bertie 'mops up the stuff'.[19] But surely, on such a question, nobody in his senses would hang a dog on the evidence of a fat-headed freak of a newt fancier who rarely drank anything but orange juice. It is also true that Bertie, impersonating Gussie, once got gloriously drunk on half a decanter of 'fine old port, full of buck and body'.[20] But surely this episode proves our contention that he was only a moderate drinker. For what heavy drinker could possibly get so tight on only half a decanter of port? (That is all Bertie drank that night, for he arrived late to find that dinner had started,[21] and was only served with orange juice in deference to Gussie's known tastes.[22]) There are many Fellows of Oxford and Cambridge Colleges who drink half a decanter of vintage port three or four nights a week without turning a hair. Incidentally, it is nice to know that Bertie did not have a hangover next morning, and was able to eat a hearty breakfast consisting of kippers, eggs and bacon, toast and marmalade and an apple.[23] This seems to confirm the old saying that if you don't mix wine with spirits, you are all right.

Bertie was a regular drinker, yes; he had a flair for the right drink for the occasion or the mood, yes;[24] but that he was a heavy drinker I strenuously deny.

BERTIE'S DRINKING: A REJOINDER
By A. D. Macintyre

Dr E. Jimpson Murgatroyd of Harley Street must join Aunt Dahlia, Gussie Fink-Nottle and G. D'Arcy ('Stilton') Cheesewright as among those who thought that Bertie drank far too much. It would be tempting to add the Rev. Aubrey Upjohn M.A. to this list. His immediate and instinctive reaction, while talking to Bertie on the telephone (a passage which ranks among the funniest pieces of short dialogue in the memoirs), is to accuse him of being intoxicated; but Mr Upjohn had formed a low opinion of Bertie while the latter was in his charge at his prep. school, Malvern House, and it would be unfair to press the point.[25] Dr Murgatroyd put the matter with medical freedom to Bertie, who denied it with 'the frank, manly statement' that some people called him 'One Martini Wooster'.[26] To this the doctor rightly paid no attention, since even on Bertie's own admission to Aunt Dahlia (see above p. 31) it underestimated his normal cocktail consumption by 100 per cent. Bertie's rebuttal of his aunt's slur was a piece of special pleading under pressure and with a hangover; and, most significantly, he omitted to tell her about the regular whisky and siphon every evening. It was the repetitive punctuality of this whisky ritual, at a time when Bertie was feeling generally out of sorts, to which he (temporarily) objected; at the end of the story 'Bertie Changes His Mind', he appears to be more or less dependent on it, watching the clock for Jeeves's appearance with the tray and referring to 'a sort of safe, restful feeling. Soothing! That's the word. Soothing!' The whisky was the final weapon by which Jeeves reduced Bertie to a kind of submission.

What are we to make of Bertie's performances in the morning? He was not an early or eager riser; the tissue-restorer was imperative if his mind was to function at all. His tissues were not usually restored by drink, so he was not a soak. On one occasion, when not suffering from a hangover, he did have two of Jeeves's specials after his morning bath and without breakfasting first (the time was, of course, near lunch).[27] I agree that there is not quite enough evidence to brand him a heavy drinker *tout court*. But he led a life which, when it took a strenuous turn, made considerable nervous demands on him. Naturally peace- and home-loving, he constantly required stimulants to meet the often horrific challenges of his life. Anyway, an active member of the Drones Club was a man not free from temptation in the matter of drink. Bertie's case was that of a regular drinker, appreciative of all kinds of drink and taking it in some quantities daily, who was also a compulsive drinker needing the stuff to rise above his dead self.[28] When others felt the need for a restorative in a crisis, he merely claimed to be 'swept along on the tide of the popular movement'; but while the others would have settled for whisky, Bertie advised port as having 'more authority', and got his way: the time is shortly after Aunt Dahlia had finished a dish of tea and a crumpet – an odd hour of the day to advise and to consume port.[29]

Much of the evidence about Bertie's drinking rests on his own statements, and he was perhaps not the best judge in his own cause. His family included at least two men who thought alcohol was a food and others, such as Uncle Cuthbert and, possibly, Uncle Willoughby, who had more or less serious drink problems. Surrounded by such examples, he naturally tried to play down his own consumption and perhaps even convinced himself that in comparison with other members of the family, he really was an 'abstemious cove'. He may have been in part a victim of heredity (cf. the case of Etienne Lantier in E. Zola, *Germinal*). Certainly there are episodes damaging to his credibility as a witness on his own drinking habits. Under Stilton Cheesewright's stiff cross-examination about Catsmeat Potter-Pirbright's party the night before, for example, he claimed to have had 'the merest sip' and to have got in at 2.30 a.m., not 3. The second part of the statement may be true. The first is incredible. Cheesewright's guess that Bertie had lowered himself to the level of the beasts of the field and behaved like a sailor in a Marseilles bistro, though over-strongly worded, must be nearer the truth. And Bertie does not trouble to rebut this particular slur or to deny Cheesewright's other strong statement: 'All you do is riot and revel and carouse'.[30] Even under Dr Murgatroyd's orders, Bertie quickly showed that he could not stay off the drink, shocking Aunt Dahlia by the way he waded into the port. True, he had an excuse.[31] He always had. His beguilingly frank admissions about the times when he had been thoroughly tight were his devices for deflecting attention from the true situation. This was summarised by Gussie Fink-Nottle who, though not himself a drinker, brought his trained scientific mind to bear on the problem: Bertie 'mops up the stuff'.[32]

BERTIE WOOSTER, GAMES PLAYER

He did not understand the first principles of Rugby football,[1] which is not surprising, since the game was not played at Eton in his day. What is surprising is that he did not evince the slightest interest in cricket – not even when there was some talk of altering the l.b.w. rule.[2] But he could recognise the M.C.C. colours when he saw them: he notes that the gardener at The Larches, Wimbledon Common, was wearing a red and yellow cap which suggested – erroneously, Bertie imagined – that he was a member of the Marylebone Cricket Club.[3] In a weak moment at Oxford, misled by his advisers, he tried to do a bit of rowing; but although he probably got into the Magdalen First Eight,[4] he gave it up because he objected to his coach's comments on the way his stomach stuck out,[5] and because he found it the deuce of a sweat.[6]

He was 16 at golf,[7] but was outed in the first round of the Drones Club's annual tournament by an unnamed blighter who had not spared himself at the luncheon table and was quite noticeably sozzled.[8] He put it across the local curate at tennis, but since we do not know how good the curate was, it is impossible to estimate Bertie's form. We do know, however, that his fast serve zipped sweetly over the net and that the man of God was utterly unable to cope with his slow, bending return down the centre line.[9] His best game was undoubtedly racquets, at which he was a blue;[10] he was also runner-up in the squash handicap at the Drones Club.[11] He was runner-up in the Drones darts tournament, and was confidently expected to win in the following year.[12] We are not told whether he did, but we do know that subsequently he cleaned up a group of pleasure-seekers at the Drones with effortless skill.[13]

He once played a distrait game of snooker pool at the Drones.[14] He does not seem to have played bridge or poker, but he once spent a restful afternoon at the Drones throwing cards into a top-hat with some of the better element.[15] He indignantly repudiates Aunt Dahlia's taunt that when he was a child he beat her at tiddlywinks because she let him, and maintains that his victories were due entirely to superior skill. 'I haven't played much tiddlywinks lately', he adds, thereby implying that he has played some.[16] He could ride a horse,[17] but never hunted; and he was a good enough shot to be invited to shoot in Norfolk, though he was so jumpy that he couldn't hit a thing.[18]

6. BERTIE AND THE FAIR SEX

I.

When we consider Bertie's attitude to the fair sex, the first thing that strikes us is his extreme susceptibility. He was not, of course, in the same league as his friends Bingo Little or Freddie Widgeon – Bingo Little, whom Bertie considered so warm-hearted that he probably had to wear asbestos vests;[1] Freddie Widgeon, of whom it was said that if all the girls he had loved and lost were placed end to end, they would reach half way down Piccadilly ('Further than that; some of them were pretty tall').[2] Bertie was not in this class, but he always had an eye for a pretty face, and was not ashamed to admit it. 'Jolly birds, girls', he might have said – but did not (though he did once say 'Jolly creatures, small girls'[3] – and lived to regret it). Apart from the twelve young ladies whom Bertie either fell for or was engaged to, and who are considered in detail below, one thinks of Mabel, the waitress in that ghastly tea-shop near the Ritz, with whom Bingo Little and Jeeves were simultaneously in love ('rather a pretty girl', thought Bertie[4]); Bingo Little's parlour-maid, who called the police and so frustrated Bertie's plan to steal the cylinder recording Mrs Little's mushy article about her husband ('not a bad-looking girl'[5]); Mary, the red-headed parlour-maid at Chuffnell Hall, who was 'full of sex appeal';[6] Queenie Silversmith, Jeeves's cousin, the parlour-maid at Deverill Hall;[7] Angelica Briscoe, the vicar's daughter at Maiden Eggesford, 'a very personable wench with whom, had I not been so preoccupied, I should probably have fallen in love';[8] and many others. He once told Gussie Fink-Nottle that he got engaged three times at Brinkley Court alone ('No business resulted, but the fact remains');[9] but he probably said this in order to nerve Gussie for the ordeal which faced him of proposing to Madeline Bassett.

The second thing that strikes us is his extreme chivalry towards women. 'At the age of six,' he says, 'I once gave my nurse a juicy one over the topknot with a porringer; since then, though few men have been more sorely tried by the sex, I have never raised my hand against a woman.'[10] Alas! the conscientious critic is obliged to point out that, when he wrote these words, Bertie must have forgotten that at their mutual dancing class, at the age of eight, incensed by some incisive remarks of Corky Pirbright about his pimples, he once forgot himself to the extent of socking her on the topknot with a wooden dumb-bell, but regretted it ever since;[11] and that, on another occasion, when Corky handed him an antique orange, 'a blue and yellow mass of pips and mildew', and bade him bung it at their instructress, who had incurred Corky's displeasure for some reason, he did it without a murmur, though knowing full well how bitter the reckoning would be.[12] He once had to remind himself that an English gentleman does not slosh a sitting red-head (Bobbie Wickham), no matter what the provocation.[13] He once came within a toucher of letting his Aunt Dahlia have it on the side of the head with a papier-mâché elephant.[14] He once actually did rap her sharply on the topknot with a paper-knife of Oriental design – and this time he shows no sign of remorse or shame.[15] But apart from this lapse, and his three childhood ones, he was, as he often tells us, a *preux chevalier*.

Bertie could not bear to see a young girl in distress, even if she was not particularly pretty, and even if he had it in for her for thwarting his plans in some way. He tells us that if you went through the W.I. postal district of London with a fine-tooth comb and a brace of bloodhounds, you wouldn't find more than about three men readier than Bertram Wooster to sympathise with a woman's distress.[16] When Aunt Agatha falsely accused a French chambermaid of stealing her pearls, the first thing Bertie noticed on entering Aunt Agatha's room was that the chambermaid was in hysterics, and almost the first thing he said was 'I say, I think there's something the matter with this girl. Isn't she crying or something?'[17]

Like the Hon. Galahad Threepwood, Bertie could not abide

sundered hearts. When Stiffy Byng's engagement to Harold ('Stinker') Pinker was temporarily broken off because he refused to pinch a policeman's helmet for her, Bertie 'ached in sympathy with her distress',[18] even though she had been guilty of some raw work even by female standards.[19] On hearing that his cousin Angela and his friend Tuppy Glossop had broken their engagement, Bertie dropped everything and rushed down to Brinkley Court to put things right, even though he had successfully resisted intense pressure from Aunt Dahlia to go there for other reasons of her own.[20] Madeline Bassett's friend Hilda Gudgeon, the 'solid girl', thwarted Bertie's plan to intercept a letter from Gussie Fink-Nottle to Madeline breaking off their engagement; yet because he knew that Hilda had had a temporary tiff with her boy friend, he 'mourned for her distress', and had he not been hiding behind a sofa, might have reached up and patted her on the head.[21]

Bertie had the most extraordinary ideas on how a gentleman should behave if he was engaged to be married, or in danger of getting into that position. In his view, it was not done for the male contracting party to break an engagement under any circumstances; but the female contracting party was not only entitled to do so, but could also reinstate herself at any time if she wanted to. And, if a girl mistakenly thought that a man was in love with her, she was entitled to propose to him whenever she liked, and the man had no option but to accept. Bertie's chivalry in allowing Florence Craye and Madeline Bassett to propose to him so frequently borders on the quixotic.

The third general point which needs to be emphasised is the extreme purity of Bertie's sexual behaviour. Sir Galahad could have taken his correspondence course. He once told Jeeves that at the age of fourteen he wrote to Marie Lloyd for her autograph, but that apart from that his private life could bear the strictest investigation.[22] He once told Pauline Stoker that he was a reputable bachelor who had never had his licence so much as endorsed[23] (whatever that may mean in this connection). As Usborne observes,[24] when Jeeves discovers that Bertie's bed has not been slept in, he does not think that Bertie is spending the night with a girl; he knows that Bertie is languishing in the cells of some police station – and he is always right.[25] When aunts or friends call upon Bertie in the morning before he has risen from his bed, it never occurs to any of them that he might be sharing that bed with some fair stranger. 'Is that young hound awake yet, Jeeves?' booms Aunt Dahlia;[26] she never asks 'Is that young hound alone this morning, Jeeves?'

When Bertie returned to his cottage at Chuffnell Regis and found Pauline Stoker in his bed and wearing his heliotrope pyjamas, he remarked: 'The attitude of fellows towards finding girls in their bedroom shortly after midnight varies. Some like it. Some don't. I didn't. I suppose it's some old Puritan strain in the Wooster blood.'[27] And when he climbed up a ladder at 1 a.m. into Florence Craye's bedroom at Brinkley Court, mistaking it for Aunt Dahlia's, and found Florence sitting up in bed in a pink boudoir cap (she was presumably also wearing a nightdress, but Bertie doesn't say so), he was so appalled at her suggestion that he wanted to kiss her softly while she slept, that he leaped perhaps six inches in the direction of the ceiling.[28] It is perhaps significant that it was not until she had had a cosy chat with Bertie, and her ex-fiancé, Stilton Cheesewright, demanded admittance in order to return her love letters, that it occurred to Florence to reach for her dressing gown.

Bertie only kissed three girls in the whole course of the Saga – and never from the usual motive. He once kissed Florence Craye in her bedroom – but only because she told him to;[29] she was not a girl whose commands it was safe to disobey. He once kissed Honoria Glossop in the park, long after their engagement was broken off – but only to make her boy friend jealous, and thus advance Sir Roderick Glossop's romance with Myrtle, Lady Chuffnell.[30] He once kissed his ex-fiancée Pauline Stoker – but only to induce her boy friend Chuffy to propose to her. This is how he described that kiss: 'Folding the girl in my arms, I got home on her right eyebrow. It wasn't one of my best, I will admit, but it was a kiss within the meaning of the Act.'[31] It sounds as though he was sadly out of practice.

Jeeves once told Pauline Stoker that Bertie was an agreeable young gentleman, but essentially one of Nature's bachelors.[32] It would have been truer to say that he was essentially one of Nature's virgins.

II

After these general reflections, we consider in more detail the appearance and characteristics of the twelve young ladies to whom Bertie was at one time engaged, or by whom he was to some extent smitten. Regretfully, we exclude his cousin Angela Travers, whom he had known since the days when he wore sailor suits and she hadn't any front teeth;[33] Zenobia ('Nobby') Hopwood, the ward of his uncle by marriage Lord Worplesdon; and Stephanie ('Stiffy') Byng, Sir Watkyn Bassett's niece, because not only was he not engaged to any of them, but also each of them was engaged to someone else – Angela to Hildebrand ('Tuppy') Glossop, Nobby to George Webster ('Boko') Fittleworth, and Stiffy to the Reverend Harold ('Stinker') Pinker. Of course it would have been contrary to that austere document, the Code of the Woosters, for Bertie to make a pass at another man's fiancée, especially when he was an old friend. He did, however, allow one of them to kiss him when she was in the grip of a more than usually high degree of emotional excitement.[34]

(i) *Florence Craye*. She was the daughter of Lord Worplesdon, and so (eventually) Bertie's cousin by marriage. She was tall and willowy and handsome, with a terrific profile, luxuriant platinum-blonde hair and bright hazel eyes.[35] But she was one of those intellectual girls,[36] steeped to the gills in serious purpose.[37] She disapproved of the Drones Club.[38] Bertie was engaged to her four times, once on his proposal and three times on hers.[39] On the first of these occasions, she took him off *Blood on the Banisters* and put him on to *Types of Ethical Theory*[40] and Tolstoy.[41] She was a female novelist, the author of *Spindrift*,[42] which went into five editions;[43] but a dramatised version failed disastrously.[44]

Jeeves disliked her because she had a tendency to be a bit imperious with the domestic staff.[45] She was, in fact, extremely bossy, and would turn down a suitor at the drop of a hat if he failed in some task which she had imposed on him, or fell below her high standards of perfection.[46] In addition to Bertie, she was engaged to Boko Fittleworth,[47] G. D'Arcy ('Stilton') Cheesewright,[48] Percy Gorringe,[49] an unnamed gentleman jockey,[50]

Harold ('Ginger') Winship[51] and a multitude of others.[52] Her ex-fiancés were numerous enough to form a club called the Old Florentians which had an annual dinner.[53] She never married.

(ii) *Muriel Singer*. She was an American chorus girl, engaged to be married to Bertie's American friend Bruce Corcoran. She heartlessly jilted him and married his uncle, Alexander Worple, instead. She is included here because, according to some shrewd critics, Bertie was never in such danger as he was when first introduced to her.[54] The point is not well taken, because Bertie would never have pinched a friend's fiancée, or allowed her to pinch him. Here is his description of her:

Muriel Singer was one of those very quiet, appealing girls who have a way of looking at you with their big eyes as if they thought you were the greatest thing on earth and wondered that you hadn't got onto it yet yourself. She sat there in a shrinking sort of way, looking at me as if she were saying to herself, 'Oh, I do hope this great strong man isn't going to hurt me'. She gave a fellow a protective kind of feeling, made him want to stroke her hand and say: 'There, there, little one!' or words to that effect. She made me feel that there was nothing I wouldn't do for her.[55]

(iii) *Honoria Glossop*. She was the only daughter of Sir Roderick Glossop, of 6B Harley Street and of Ditteredge Hall in Hampshire. She had been at Girton where, in addition to enlarging her brain to the most frightful extent, she had gone in for every kind of sport and developed the physique of a middle-weight catch-as-catch-can wrestler. Bertie wasn't sure she didn't box for the University when she was up.[56] She was the sort of girl who reduces you to pulp with sixteen sets of tennis and a few rounds of golf, and then comes down to dinner as fresh as a daisy, expecting you to take an intelligent interest in Freud.[57] She also read Nietzsche[58] and had a penetrating laugh, variously described as like the Scotch express going under a bridge,[59] a squadron of cavalry charging over a tin bridge,[60] waves breaking on a stern and rock-bound coast[61] and a steam-riveting machine.[62]

She was Aunt Agatha's selection as the future Mrs Bertram Wooster,[63] but although Bertie was engaged to her for a week or two, it was due to a misunderstanding. Bingo Little was in love with her, so Bertie tried to plead his friend's cause in words which can only be described as a masterpiece of tactlessness: 'It may sound rummy and all that, but there's somebody who's frightfully in love with you and so forth – a friend of mine, you know'.[64] Honoria, thinking that Bertie was proposing marriage on his own account, accepted him, but Jeeves managed to extricate him by sedulously fostering her father's notion that he (Bertie) was insane.[65]

In a fit of absentmindedness, Bertie's old friend Charles Edward Biffen got engaged to Honoria. The news of this gave Bertie 'a peculiar feeling': he compares himself to a man strolling through the jungle with a boyhood chum, who meets a tigress or a jaguar, manages to shin up a tree and looks down and sees the friend of his youth vanishing into the undergrowth in the animal's slavering jaws.[66]

Honoria eventually married an angry young novelist named Blair Eggleston. Bertie and Aunt Dahlia agreed that they both had it coming to them.[67]

(iv) *Aline Hemmingway*. Bertie met her on the Blue Train, helped her with her baggage, got into conversation with her, and had a bite of dinner with her in the restaurant car.[68] He thought she was the sweetest girl in the world.[69] It turned out that she and her brother Sidney, who masqueraded as a parson, were international jewel thieves. They tried to steal Aunt Agatha's pearls, and would have succeeded but for some quick thinking on Jeeves's part. Aunt Agatha accused the chambermaid of stealing them, so Bertie was able to put it across her properly[70] – all the more so since she had encouraged his budding romance with Aline:[71] but this aspect of the matter was suppressed when the story was republished in the Omnibus edition.

(v) *Heloise Pringle*. She was the daughter of Professor Pringle of Cambridge, a cousin of Honoria Glossop, and a childhood friend of Oliver Sipperley, who had not seen her since he was ten, fourteen years earlier. Bertie went to stay with the Pringles, impersonating Oliver, who had been sentenced to thirty days without the option for pinching a policeman's helmet on Boat Race night.[72] During his visit, Heloise began to haunt Bertie. She tried to improve his mind, and begged him to give up smoking and his supposed friendship with Bertie Wooster.[73] She tried to make him kiss her by reminding him that when they (i.e. she and Oliver) were children together, he cried because she was cross and wouldn't let him do so. With her shoulder squashing against his and her back hair tickling his nose, a perfectly loony impulse came sweeping over him to kiss her, but he was saved at the last moment by a goddess out of the machine, heavily disguised as Aunt Jane, aged 86.[74]

(vi) *Cynthia Wickhammersley*. She was the youngest daughter of the Earl of Wickhammersley, of Twing Hall, Gloucestershire, a great pal of Bertie's father when he was alive. Bertie knew her since she was seven. She was a dashed pretty and lively and attractive girl, but full of ideals and all that.[75] There was a time when Bertie thought he was in love with her, but when he proposed she nearly laughed herself into a permanent state of hiccoughs.[76] Later, Bingo Little was in love with her, but she married the Reverend James Bates, who won the Great Sermon Handicap.[77] He was perhaps fortunate to win that classic event, because if the Stewards had known that he had borrowed his uncle's 50-minute sermon on Brotherly Love, he must surely have been disqualified for boring.

(vii) *Gwladys Pendlebury*. She was an artist whom Bertie met at a party in Chelsea. She painted Bertie's portrait, but it gave him a distinctly hungry look. Aunt Dahlia expressed her astonishment that Bertie hadn't enough sense to steer clear of anything labelled Gwladys or Ysobel or Ethyl or Mabelle or Kathryn – but particularly Gwladys.[78] She eventually married Lucius Pim, another artist, who had wavy hair.[79]

(viii) *Roberta ('Bobbie') Wickham*. She was the daughter of the late Sir Cuthbert and of Lady Wickham, of Skeldings Hall, Hertfordshire. She appears in three Jeeves short stories (nos. 23, 25, 27), one Jeeves novel (*Joy in the Morning*), three Mulliner stories (nos. 16, 17, 18), and one other short story,[80] so there is plenty of data about her. There is no doubt that Wodehouse loved her as much as he loved Sue Brown, Aunt Dahlia, Ukridge, Psmith and Uncle Fred. She imparted fizz and sparkle to the stories, because she had a lively sense of humour, was a keen practical joker, and was always trying to start something. She usually succeeded.

In appearance she was a slim, boyish-looking girl with bright red shingled hair.[81] She 'resembled a particularly good-looking schoolboy who had dressed up in his sister's clothes'.[82] She drove a fast motor-car very fast indeed to the danger of the public, and was always getting fined for driving down Piccadilly at 40 m.p.h.;[83] once she smashed up the car while it was uninsured.[84] She had a great number of suitors, including Bertie, who was crazy about her at one time.[85] He proposed to her several times, but she declined to co-operate, laughed like a bursting paper bag and told him not to be a silly ass.[86]

Jeeves disapproved of her. He thought she was frivolous, volatile and lacking in seriousness.[87] Eventually he managed to persuade Bertie that she was a 'carrot-topped Jezebel',[88] who was 'capable of double-crossing a strong man's honest love'.[89] Several times Jeeves said to Bertie 'Miss Wickham, though a charming young lady –',[90] but he was never allowed to finish the sentence.

On one occasion she tried to soften up her mother to her impending engagement to Reggie ('Kipper') Herring by inserting an announcement in *The Times* of her engagement to Bertie, without troubling to inform either him[91] or Kipper[92] that she had done so. There were no flies on Miss Wickham: the only young man who had no illusions about her was her neighbour Algernon Crufts in Hertfordshire; he once called her a chump to her face.[93] One wonders what her married life with Kipper can have been like.

(ix) *Pauline Stoker*. She was the daughter of J. Washburn Stoker, an American multi-millionaire. Bertie says that she was one of the most beautiful girls he had ever met,[94] that she was darkish in her general colour scheme, and that her beauty maddened him like wine.[95] They met in the course of some beano at the Sherry-Netherland Hotel in New York.[96] During his brief courtship, Bertie's car broke down one night and they were stranded for hours somewhere in the wilds of Westchester County. It was raining and her feet got wet, so Bertie (very wisely, so he says) took her stockings off to prevent her catching cold.[97] Two weeks after they first met, Bertie proposed at the Plaza Hotel[98] and was accepted.[99] He did not kiss her, because a waiter came into the room with a tray of beef sandwiches and the moment passed.[100] Alas! the engagement only lasted two days, during most of which time Bertie was in bed with a nasty cold.[101] Then Pauline, under pressure from her father, broke off the engagement by letter, because Sir Roderick Glossop told him that Bertie was 'barmy to the core'.[102] Bertie often wondered what on earth made Pauline accept him.[103] She told him later that it was because 'there's a sort of woolly-headed duckiness about you',[104] thus revealing herself as quite a penetrating student of the psychology of the individual. She married Bertie's friend Chuffy, Lord Chuffnell.

(x) *Madeline Bassett.* She was the daughter of Sir Watkyn Bassett, J.P. She was pretty enough in a droopy, blonde, saucer-eyed way,[105] being slim and svelte and bountifully equipped with golden hair and all the fixings.[106] But she had grave defects. She thought that the stars were God's daisy chain;[107] that every time a fairy shed a tear, a star was born in the Milky Way;[108] that rabbits were gnomes in attendance on the Fairy Queen;[109] and that wreaths of mist on the grass were elves' bridal veils.[110] She was a droopy, soupy, sloppy, squashy, mushy, sentimental Gawd-help us with melting eyes and a cooing voice.[111] Her favourite reading was Christopher Robin, Winnie the Pooh[112] and *Mervyn Keene, Clubman* (Rosie M. Banks' masterpiece).[113] She was incapable of preparing the simplest meal.[114] Bertie does not hesitate to describe her as 'a ghastly girl'[115] and 'England's premier pill'.[116] ('The Woosters are chivalrous, but they can speak their minds.')

She was convinced that Bertie was in love with her because in a rash moment he offered to press Gussie Fink-Nottle's suit, and she misinterpreted his remarks.[117] She was engaged several times to Gussie, who eventually saw the light and eloped with the cook.[118] She offered four times to be Bertie's wife, and he, because of his extraordinary Code, had no choice but to accept her.[119] She eventually married Roderick Spode, seventh Earl of Sidcup, the human gorilla.[120] This delighted her father, who said that this was one of the oldest titles in England.[121] If he was right, the other six earls must have broken all records for longevity. Perhaps the ancient Saxon earldom was called out of abeyance in the eighteenth century.

(xi) *Cora ('Corky') Pirbright.* She was a Hollywood film star whose screen name was Cora Starr. She came from a theatrical family: her father wrote the music for *The Blue Lady* and other substantial hits; her mother was the New York star Elsie Cattermole; her brother was the West End actor Claude Cattermole ('Catsmeat') Potter-Pirbright, a friend of Bertie's.[122] Her uncle was the vicar of King's Deverill in Hampshire.[123] Bertie had known her on and off ever since they were kids and attended the same dancing class. She was one of those lissom girls of medium height and her map had always been worth more than a passing glance. Her eyes were a kind of browny hazel and her hair rather along the same lines. The general effect was that of an angel who ate a lot of yeast.[124] Catsmeat reminds Bertie that he was making a colossal ass of himself over her at one time; and Bertie admits it.[125] She married Esmond Haddock, the handsome young squire of Deverill Hall.

(xii) *Vanessa Cook*. Bertie met her at a cocktail party, and such was her radiant beauty that it was only a couple of minutes later that he was saying to himself, 'Bertram, this is a good thing. Push it along'. In due course he suggested a merger, but no business resulted. This was just as well, for she was always going on protest marches, and not at all a suitable mate for Bertie. A year later she was engaged to Orlo Porter, who was on the same staircase as Bertie at Magdalen, but in no sense a buddy of his, being a Communist and also a protest-marcher.[126] Vanessa's cool assumption that she had only got to state her wishes and all and sundry would jump to fulfil them gave Bertie the pip.[127] After a quarrel with Orlo she tells Bertie she will be his wife, but that he must give up smoking and cocktails, read improving books,[128] and resign from the Drones Club.[129] But in the end she elopes with Orlo, so all is well.

III.

Few passages in the Saga throw a more revealing light on Bertie's attitude to girls than his reaction to discovering Pauline Stoker in his bed at midnight and wearing his heliotrope pyjamas.[130] Although he thought she looked fine in that slumberwear, he chatted her up for half an hour and then left her to spend the rest of the night in his two-seater without even kissing her goodnight. And much good did his delicacy do him, for he was first hounded by the over-zealous local constabulary, and then had to face two painful interviews, one with Pauline's fiancé Lord Chuffnell, the other with her father, each of whom suspected that the worst had happened. Of course with any other man than Bertie, their suspicions would have been amply justified. But not with Bertie.

What motive can Pauline have had in involving Bertie in this embarrassing situation? She was incarcerated in her father's yacht, because he thought she was still in love with Bertie and he wanted to prevent her meeting him. So she swam ashore in her swimming suit, hoping to lie low and get clothes (from whom?) so that she could visit Lord Chuffnell at the Hall. Now Pauline had been engaged to Bertie for only two days, and known him for only two weeks before that: long enough perhaps for her to realise that he was a chump, but hardly long enough to realise that he was a *preux chevalier* and as innocent as the babe unborn in his sexual approach to women. She must have been a chump of the first water herself – a far bigger chump than Bertie – if she supposed that the best route to her fiancé's heart was via her ex-fiancé's bedroom. But this is exactly what she did suppose, for when Chuffy came and put Bertie to bed and found her there, and she saw what he suspected, she blushed crimson and a dickens of a row ensued.[131]

And what about Jeeves's part in this sad affair? The more closely we examine it, the more dubious his behaviour becomes. We know that he could be singularly ruthless at times. He once struck Oliver Sipperley a sharp blow on the head with Bertie's putter.[132] He once coshed P.C. Dobbs to prevent him arresting Gussie Fink-Nottle; and Bertie wondered what would be his own fate, next time there was a difference of opinion between him and Jeeves at Wooster GHQ over purple socks, white mess-jackets or soft-bosomed evening shirts.[133] Sure enough, Jeeves did strike Bertie a violent blow on the back hair with a gong stick;[134] and he once rendered the unspeakable Bingley (or Brinkley), Moscow's pride, temporarily insensible by inserting a chemical substance in his beverage.[135] But on this occasion his methods were far more subtle. For Jeeves was living on Pop Stoker's yacht, and no doubt feeding almost exclusively on fish. Can we really believe that he could not have thought of half a dozen schemes for facilitating Pauline's escape from durance vile, other than the clumsy one which she devised and he approved? Bertie was amazed that Jeeves didn't try to stop her; instead, 'he said you would be delighted to help me', she told Bertie.[136] Is it not more likely that Jeeves deliberately planted Pauline in Bertie's bed? What his motives were, we can only guess. He may have considered Pauline a less unsuitable mate than any of the other girls with whom Bertie was from time to time involved, and that, being no longer in Bertie's employment, he had nothing to lose from Bertie's marriage – certainly not the indignity of being sacked by Bertie's wife. He may have been sorry for Bertie's perennially sex-starved state, and thought it was time he had a little fun. Or (and this seems the most likely explanation) he may have thought it would be funny to plant a girl in Bertie's bed, and see what happened. When no business resulted, he must have been a disappointed man.

One shudders to think of the risks which Jeeves made Pauline run, simply in order to gratify his Rabelaisian sense of humour. She might have had a fit of cramp and been drowned before she reached the shore. She might have caught her death of cold after her long swim in the dark cold sea. She might have cut herself to pieces, climbing in through Bertie's cottage window. She might have lost her virtue (Jeeves hoped she would). When one adds to Jeeves's cynical disregard of Pauline's physical and moral welfare his utter disloyalty to his employer (her fiancé), we must conclude that no blacker fiend has ever sullied the pages of English literature. Iago could have taken his correspondence course.

7. BERTIE'S CARS

I.

Bertie's car was kept at a garage near his flat in Berkeley Square.[1] We are told many times that it was a two-seater[2] and (less often) a sports model;[3] and we also know that it had six cylinders[4] and a bulb horn.[5] The dickey was large enough to accommodate two passengers on short journeys,[6] but not large enough comfortably to accommodate Jeeves and the luggage required by Bertie and Jeeves for a short visit to Steeple Bumpleigh in Hampshire.[7]

What make was this car? Bertie once says it was a Widgeon Seven,[8] but I think he must have been mistaken. For if 'Seven' refers to its horse-power, it cannot have had six cylinders; and if 'Widgeon' means 'Austin', it cannot have had a bulb horn or been a two-seater, because Austin Sevens did not have bulb horns and there was no two-seater model. Bertie may of course have changed his car during the five years spanned by the Saga, but there is no evidence that he ever did. Moreover, it was the alleged Widgeon Seven which had the bulb horn and is described as a two-seater, so even if he did change his car, our problem is not solved. On the whole, it seems safer to conclude that he had but one, and that, while it may have been a Widgeon, it was certainly not a Seven.

There is a further problem. When Jeeves was driving Bertie back to London from Brighton, a hitch hiker thumbed a lift. She turned out to be Miss Peggy Mainwaring, aged twelve, who was playing truant from her school. 'She climbed in at the back, let down one of the spare seats, and knelt on it to facilitate conversation.' She said she thought the car was a Sunbeam, and neither Jeeves nor Bertie contradicted her.[9] Later Bertie sprang with almost incredible nimbleness into the tonneau (not the dickey), lay on the floor and covered himself with a rug.[10] This car sounds much larger and more stately than a two-seater or a sports model, for what dickey ever had two spare folding seats? What is the explanation of this discrepancy? I think it is very simple. Bertie had had a slight attack of influenza,[11] so (I suggest) Jeeves seized the opportunity to have the two-seater serviced (it probably needed decarbonising). This took a little longer than expected, so when they decided to go to Brighton for a few days, Jeeves had to hire a car. This theory also explains why Jeeves and not Bertie took the wheel for the only time in the Saga; evidently the garage had a strict rule that only the man who signed the papers was permitted to drive.

Jeeves once ventured to criticise Bertie's driving: 'If I might make the suggestion, sir, I should not jerk the steering wheel with quite such suddenness. We nearly collided with that omnibus.'[12] Bertie knew nothing about the mechanism of a car; when it broke down, his talents were limited to twisting the wheel and tooting the tooter.[13] And in its later days it did sometimes break down: it did so on the way from London to King's Deverill in Hampshire,[14] from Steeple Bumpleigh to East Wibley in Hampshire;[15] and from Brinkley Court in Worcestershire to Herne Bay in Kent, when it had to be towed to a garage.[16]

Bertie was generous in lending his car to Jeeves or to friends. He lent it to his cousin Claude, so that Claude could drive to Southampton and catch the boat to South Africa without any risk of meeting his brother Eustace, who was catching the boat train at Waterloo.[17] He lent it to Bingo Little, so that Bingo could drive Jeeves back from Lakenham races.[18] He lent it to Gussie Fink-Nottle, so that Gussie could escape from Totleigh Towers and the wrath of Sir Watkyn Bassett.[19] Three times in ten pages he lent it to Catsmeat Potter-Pirbright, so that Catsmeat could go to London and consult Jeeves, take Jeeves's cousin Queenie Silversmith to the pictures at Basingstoke, and go to Wimbledon Common to prevent Madeline Bassett from visiting Deverill Hall.[20] He twice lent it to Jeeves.[21]

II.

Bertie once hired a car to drive from Cambridge to Beckley-on-the-Moor in Yorkshire. He accepted without question Jeeves's statement that it was 'our best plan'.[22] This episode throws a revealing but somewhat murky light on Jeeves's character. For in the first place it is not the best route from Cambridge to Yorkshire. We are not told where Beckley-on-the-Moor was, but it cannot have been very far from York, because Jeeves told Bertie that the distance was about 150 miles, and York is 151 miles from Cambridge. Surely the best plan would have been to take a train from Cambridge to the G.N.R. main line at Huntingdon (a mere 16 miles), take a fast train from there to York, and hire a car at York if there was no convenient train or bus. And, even if it was the best route in normal circumstances, it certainly was not so in the circumstances which confronted Bertie. Let us consider his situation: he was staying with total strangers at Cambridge, impersonating his friend Oliver Sipperley, who had been sentenced to thirty days in prison for pinching a policeman's helmet on Boat Race night. The household consisted of Professor Pringle – a 'thinnish, baldish, dyspeptic-lookingish cove with an eye like a haddock'; his wife, who looked as though she had had bad news round about the year 1900 and never really got over it; his mother; his aunt Jane, aged eighty-six;[23] and his daughter Heloise, who was determined to trap Bertie into matrimony, and being even brainier than her cousin Honoria Glossop, was quite likely to succeed.[24] And one evening Sir Roderick Glossop came to dinner and denounced Bertie as an impostor, thus rendering immediate flight his only course.[25] One would think he would not have wanted to revisit Cambridge for many a long day. And yet, thanks to Jeeves, he had to do so, and to remain there at least one more night. For in those days there were no nation-wide car-hire firms with branches in every large town; if you wanted to hire a car, you had to return it to the garage from which you hired it.

So what can have been Jeeves's motive in telling Bertie that 'our best plan would be to hire a car' and thus ensure that they paid a return visit to Cambridge? Obviously, he must have had some business of his own in Cambridge, some scheme or plan which required another day or two there to bring it to fruition. This theory accords well with the intense pressure which Jeeves brought to bear on Bertie to induce him to go to Cambridge and impersonate Oliver Sipperley. Although he was in the throes of a severe hangover, Bertie could see that Jeeves's plan was a loony one – pure banana oil. 'It is not like you to come into the presence of a sick man and gibber,' he said. It took Jeeves a quarter of an hour, instead of the usual five minutes, to reason Bertie into acceptance of his plan, which Bertie considered 'the weirdest to date'; and Jeeves only clinched the thing by telling Bertie that his Aunt Agatha, having read about the police court proceedings in the evening paper, was out with her hatchet.[26]

What business had Jeeves in Cambridge which demanded his presence there for one more night? I see no reason to reject the obvious explanation that he was pursuing some girl whose resistance he had not yet overcome. I do not think that he was any more immune from tender passion than the next man. Bertie would naturally gloss over this side of Jeeves's character, partly out of loyalty to Jeeves, and partly because 'the Woosters do not bandy a woman's name'. But still, there are hints here and there in Bertie's narrative that Jeeves liked girls. In one story, Jeeves tried hard to persuade Bertie to go on a round-the-world cruise on which Jeeves had set his heart; and Bertie thought that someone must have been telling Jeeves about the dancing girls of Bali.[27] In another story, Jeeves, while on holiday at Herne Bay, was invited to judge a bathing belles contest at Folkestone ('all most attractive young ladies', he told Bertie).[28] Besides, is it likely that a man of Jeeves's virile and ruthless personality would have been content to spend his leisure hours curled up with Spinoza's latest, or playing bridge at the Junior Ganymede club, or shrimping at Bognor or Herne Bay?

Of one thing we may be quite sure, and that is that Jeeves's approach to the fair sex must have ben quite different from Bertie's. Bertie was meek and gentle, chivalrous to a fault, and a *preux chevalier*. Jeeves would not have flitted vapidly and ineffectively from flower to flower, nor allowed a girl he thought he was finished with from re-entering his life like a recurring decimal. On the contrary, having marked down his prey, he would have pursued her with relentless cunning, and would not have hesitated to cosh her on the head, or lace her drink, in order to achieve his ends. Did he entertain his girl friends in Bertie's flat? I think it very probable that he did, for the risk of discovery must have been remote. Bertie never entered Jeeves's bedroom (though he once banged on the door in the middle of the night because he urgently needed advice and sympathy, and Jeeves emerged in a brown dressing-gown[29]). Bertie often dined out at the Drones club or elsewhere, and went to a musical comedy or a night-club (he was a member of half a dozen of them[30]). There was always the chance that he would return so drunk as to be incapable of distinguishing between the standard lamp and a burglar.[31] And even if he came in sober, Jeeves would have had no difficulty in convincing him that the young lady Jeeves was entertaining had come from Debenhams or Libertys to match the kitchen curtains. And, of course, there was never any risk that Bertie would discover her presence in the morning, because he never surfaced before 10 a.m. at the earliest, and nothing made any sense to him before he had had his tea.

Who was the girl whom Jeeves was pursuing at Cambridge? I think she may well have been Mabel, the Camberwell beauty. For Mabel, you remember, was loved not only by Bingo Little but also by Jeeves. She was not a mere passive recipient of Bingo's admiration: she tried to 'push it along' by giving him a crimson satin tie decorated with horseshoes.[32] Evidently, she wanted to better herself by marrying out of her class. When her romance with Bingo came unstuck, and Jeeves was pressing his unwelcome attentions on her, what more natural than that she should give up her job at the tea-shop, and take another at the University Arms in Cambridge?

8. JEEVES'S SARTORIAL TYRANNIES

Jeeves was undoubtedly a domestic tyrant. He rules Bertie with a rod of iron, especially when Bertie sported anything in the least out of the ordinary in the matter of dress. Many of the stories begin with Bertie attempting to assert himself; he has a painful scene with Jeeves, who appears to accept the situation, but always gets his way in the end. Jeeves's technique varies: sometimes he gives the offending garments away without Bertie's knowledge or consent;[1] sometimes he sends them back to the shop from which Bertie ordered them;[2] sometimes he deliberately injures them beyond repair;[3] sometimes Bertie, weakened by relief and gratitude, gives in and tells Jeeves to dispose of them.[4] The most poignant of these occasions was when Bertie, having bought a white mess jacket at Cannes which Jeeves considered quite unsuitable, appealed to Jeeves to extricate him from the clutches of Madeline Bassett, but before doing so made it quite clear that if he was successful there must be 'no rot about that white mess jacket'.[5] Yet Jeeves, the low hound, deliberately burnt it while ironing it, and did so so thoroughly that Bertie could not wear it again.[6] One is sometimes surprised that Bertie considered this sort of treachery a lesser evil than having to marry Madeline Bassett. The mystery deepens when we consider that in one of the stories Jeeves, on temporary loan from Bertie, takes service as a butler with an impecunious peer who tries to restore the family fortunes by working as a bookie. Jeeves accompanies him to Epsom Downs as his clerk, dressed in a check suit and wearing a false moustache[7] – scarcely a judicious addition to the afternoon costume of a gentleman's personal gentleman.[8] As Bertie said when he discovered that Jeeves, after making heavy weather of 'a perfectly ordinary white mess jacket', incited Gussie Fink-Nottle to go to a fancy dress dance in scarlet tights as Mephistopheles, one looks askance at this in-and-out running.[9]

The full tale of Jeeves's sartorial tyrannies is as follows:

The Tyranny of the Check Suit.[10]
The Tyranny of the Scarlet Cummerbund.[11]
The Tyranny of the Purple Socks.[12]
The Tyranny of the Broadway Special Hat and the Pink Tie.[13]
The Tyranny of the Old Etonian Spats.[14]
The Tyranny of the Soft-Bosomed Dress Shirts.[15]
The Tyranny of the Polychromatic Plus Fours.[16]
The Tyranny of the White Mess Jacket.[17]
The Tyranny of the Blue Alpine Hat.[18]

FOUR WOOSTER MYSTERIES

I. THE MYSTERY OF THE THIRD DINNER JACKET

'Do you dress for dinner every night, Bertie?'
'Jeeves,' I said coldly. 'How many suits of evening clothes have we?'
'We have three suits of full evening dress, sir; two dinner jackets – '
'Three.'
'For practical purposes two only, sir. If you remember, we cannot wear the third.'[1]

It is tempting to suppose that this third dinner jacket was the one Bertie was wearing on that memorable evening after dinner at the Drones, when Tuppy Glossop bet him he couldn't swing himself across the swimming bath by the ropes and rings; and when Bertie came to the last ring he found that Tuppy had looped it back against the rail, leaving Bertie with no alternative but to drop into the water. The first time Bertie tells this story to Jeeves, there is no mention of any dinner jacket.[2] But the third time that he tells it, he reminds Jeeves that he had the job of drying and pressing his dress clothes afterwards.[3] There is an obvious discrepancy here, unless we assume that after the incident Bertie was so chagrined that he hadn't the nerve to tell Jeeves what had happened, but merely handed over his dress clothes to be dried and pressed. But in that case, how did he account to Jeeves for their wetness?

II. WHO COOKED BERTIE'S BREAKFAST?

In *Thank You, Jeeves*, Bertie went to the Alhambra and, fascinated by the extreme virtuosity of Ben Bloom and his Sixteen Baltimore

Buddies, bought a banjolele and practised playing it in his London flat. All the other tenants complained, and the management gave him the option to cease playing the banjolele or quit. Bertie decided to quit, take a cottage in the country and continue playing the instrument there, whereupon Jeeves gave notice.

Bertie rented a cottage at Chuffnell Regis in Somerset from his old friend Lord Chuffnell ('Chuffy'). He gave his new man, Brinkley, the evening off and drove to Bristol for dinner and a musical comedy. Brinkley stayed out all night and did not return till 9.30 p.m. the following night, when, stewed to the gills after the toot of a lifetime, he burned down the cottage.

When Bertie returned from Bristol at midnight, he found his ex-fiancée Pauline Stoker in his bed, wearing his heliotrope pyjamas. Shying away from this apparition, Bertie tried to sleep first in his car and then in the tool-shed, much impeded by constant visits from the over-zealous Sergeant Voules and P.C. Dobson. They invoked the assistance of Chuffy, Pauline's current fiancé, who, jumping to the conclusion that Bertie was as tight as an owl, insisted on putting him to bed. When he found Pauline there, a dickens of a row ensued, Chuffy withdrew in a dudgeon, Pauline returned to her father's yacht, and Bertie went to sleep in his own bed, after a painful interview with Pauline's father, who strongly disapproved of him.

It was about ten-thirty on a fine summer morning, and the sunshine streaming in through the window seemed to be calling me to get up and see what I could do to an egg, a rasher, and the good old pot of coffee. I had a hasty bath and shave and trotted down to the kitchen, full of *joie de vivre*. It was not until I had finished breakfast and was playing the banjolele in the front garden that something seemed to whisper reproachfully in my ear that I had no right to be feeling as perky as this on what was essentially the morning after.[4]

The mystery is – who cooked Bertie's breakfast? And, since 'bathrooms were not provided in Chuffy's little homes',[5] where did he have his bath?

III. Bertie's London Address

In one of the early stories, Bertie says that the address of his
London flat was 6a, Crichton Mansions, Berkeley Street, W.1.[6]
But in three much later stories, his address is Berkeley Mansions,
Berkeley Square.[7] When did he move, and why?

It is tempting to suppose that when he returned to London
after his cottage at Chuffnell Regis and all its contents (including
the banjolele) were destroyed by fire, the pride which he inherited
from his crusading ancestors prevented him from cringing to the
management of his old flat, and so he had to take his custom
elsewhere. Or perhaps he merely found that they had relet the
flat.

But this explanation will not do, because at the beginning of
the story in which his cottage burns down, Bertie had already
changed his London address. So the mystery remains.

IV. The Reconciliations with Sir Roderick Glossop

The long story *Thank You, Jeeves* opens with Bertie seething
with rage against his old enemy Sir Roderick Glossop, the eminent nerve specialist or loony-doctor, who had recently caused
Bertie's engagement to Pauline Stoker to be broken off by in-
forming Pauline's father that he (Bertie) was insane.[8] It ends
with Bertie and Sir Roderick reconciled at last, even to the extent
of Bertie calling him Roddy.[9] The cause of this reconciliation
was that they had both blacked their faces, Bertie with boot
polish, Sir Roderick with burnt cork, and spent a night of terror
wandering round Chuffnell Regis with no place to lay their
heads.[10] This reconciliation was no mere flash in the pan, for in
a later short story, Bertie goes to considerable trouble and ex-
pense, and even runs the appalling risk of getting engaged again
to Sir Roderick's daughter Honoria, in order to further Sir
Roderick's romance with Myrtle, Lady Chuffnell. (He gave Honoria 'the rush of a lifetime' and even kissed her in the park.[11])

The Code of the Woosters is a later story than *Thank You,*

Jeeves, and *Jeeves in the Offing* is a later story than *The Code of the Woosters*, because each contains references to events occurring in the previous one.[12] Therefore, *Jeeves in the Offing* must be a later story than *Thank You, Jeeves*. Yet, at the beginning of *Jeeves in the Offing*, when Aunt Dahlia announces that she is lunching with Sir Roderick Glossop, Bertie is surprised and says he 'would not have cared to lunch with him myself' because their relations were 'on the stiff side'.[13] Sir Roderick Glossop masquerades as Aunt Dahlia's butler under the unlikely name of Swordfish.[14] Half-way through the story, Bertie and Sir Roderick are reconciled again, and start calling each other Roddy and Bertie.[15] The cause of this reconciliation was their mutual discovery that they had stolen biscuits from the head-master's study when at their prep. schools.[16]

One can only suppose that, in the interval between *Thank You, Jeeves* and *Jeeves in the Offing*, Bertie and Sir Roderick had another row. The mystery is, what was it about?

10. WHERE IS KING'S DEVERILL?

Easby in Shropshire, Brinkley Court in Worcestershire, Twing Hall and Totleigh Towers in Gloucestershire, Woollam Chersey and Skeldings Hall in Hertfordshire, Ditteredge Hall, Bleaching Court, Marsham Manor, Deverill Hall and Bumpleigh Hall in Hampshire, Chuffnell Hall and Eggesford Hall in Somerset – these are the country houses which Bertie stayed at, or visited for a meal. But where are they? In most cases, we are merely told which county they are in. We also know that Brinkley Court is near Droitwich[1] and that Chuffnell Regis is on the coast about thirty miles from Bristol,[2] which enables us to pinpoint it fairly exactly. Burnham-on-Sea, which is twenty-seven miles from Bristol, seems to fill the bill quite nicely. It has a river harbour which is well buoyed and lighted, and has an outer anchorage which, though a little exposed to the west at high water, has depths of up to eight feet at low water in places – deep enough no doubt for Pop Stoker's motor yacht. (These unfortunate specimens of marine architecture draw very little, however big they are.)

The critic Howarth points out that we ought to be able to pinpoint Deverill Hall too, because of the evidence of Dame Daphne Winkworth's yell, the evidence of the Lovers' Leap, and the evidence of the railway journeys.

Deverill Hall is a fine old pile, built in Tudor times, with battlements and all the fixings, such as spreading lawns, gay flower beds, gravel soil and spreading views. It was the home of Esmond Haddock, his five aunts, and his cousin Gertrude Winkworth. It is within walking distance of the village of King's Deverill, which has a vicarage, a post office, a village hall (built in 1881), a public house (the Goose and Cowslip) and several picturesque cottages, one of which is the police station.

Now let us look at the evidence about its location:

(i) *The evidence of the yell.* Catsmeat Potter-Pirbright was a friend of Bertie's, a well-known member of the Drones Club, and a West End actor. He met Gertrude Winkworth when they were both staying at a house in Norfolk, and got engaged to her. When she returned to Deverill Hall to break the news to her mother, Dame Daphne Winkworth, the parent (not fancying an actor for a son-in-law) 'let out a yell you could have heard at Basingstoke' which, Catsmeat told Bertie, was about twenty miles away as the crow flies.[3] It is important to notice that Catsmeat did not hear this yell. He told Bertie that he hadn't yet met any of the aunts.[4] He did not go to Deverill Hall until later, when he pretended to be Meadowes, Bertie's man.[5] If he had been there before, he would surely have been denounced as an impostor.

(ii) *The evidence of the Lovers' Leap.* Gertrude wrote and told Catsmeat that her cousin Esmond Haddock was giving her 'the rush of a lifetime'; and Catsmeat, hearing that Bertie was about to visit Deverill Hall, urged him to start 'busting up Esmond's sinister game'. He told Bertie that Esmond's most recent suggestion was that Gertrude and Esmond should 'take sandwiches and ride out to a place about fifteen miles away, where there are cliffs and things', and show her the Lovers' Leap. 'Fifteen miles there, then the Lovers' Leap, then fifteen miles back. The imagination reels at the thought of what excesses a fellow like Esmond Haddock may commit on a thirty-mile ride with a Lovers' Leap thrown in half way.'[6] The evidence could hardly be more precise that this Lovers' Leap was fifteen miles from Deverill Hall. Catsmeat says so three times, and to make his meaning abundantly plain, also gives quite correctly the distance there and back. No room for a misunderstanding here, surely.

(iii) *The evidence of the railway journeys.* Bertie drove alone to Deverill Hall in his two-seater, having presumably told Jeeves to follow by train with the luggage. The car broke down half way through the journey, so it was getting on for eight when he arrived.[7] Dame Daphne Winkworth sent him to bed early with a flea in his ear because he got drunk with Esmond Haddock over the port.[8] Catsmeat arrived during dinner, pretending to be

Meadowes, Bertie's man.[9] Gussie Fink-Nottle and Jeeves arrived together at a somewhat late hour in the night.[10] Catsmeat must have come by train, because he later borrowed Bertie's car on three occasions.[11] Gussie, on the other hand, had his car with him,[12] so he must have driven down with Jeeves.

In order to intercept a letter from Gussie breaking his engagement to Madeline Bassett, Bertie caught the 2.54 a.m. milk train from King's Deverill to Wimbledon,[13] and returned by train later in the same day. Here is his description of his return journey: 'You change twice before you get to Basingstoke and then change again and take the branch line. And once you're on the branch line, it's quicker to walk.'[14]

The critic Howarth says (and I agree) that the first two of these changes must have been at Surbiton and Woking, and that from Basingstoke onwards the plot thickens. He says that the L.S.W.R. main line divides beyond Basingstoke, and that King's Deverill, being on a branch line, could not have been on the Winchester and Southampton line nor on the line to Andover and Salisbury, and that this rules out a fair slice of Hampshire. Again, I agree. It could not, he says, have been on the old G.W.R. line from Basingstoke to Reading, because that was in the wrong direction altogether for Lovers' Leaps. So it must have been on the only other branch line out of Basingstoke, the long-abandoned single-track branch line to Alton. The difficulty is that Alton is only nine miles as the crow flies from Basingstoke. It is true (says Howarth) that another branch line leads thence to Privett, Meonstoke and Fareham, and that a crow, exhausted after his twenty-mile stint, would have got to Meonstoke. But he rejects the possibility that King's Deverill was near Meonstoke on the ground (plausible at first sight) that no one would have approached it via Basingstoke, when he could have caught a through train to Alton at Surbiton or Woking. He concludes that Catsmeat grossly exaggerated the distance over which Dame Daphne Winkworth's yell was audible, and that King's Deverill was somewhere near Preston Candover (I think he means Cliddesden) or Herriard or Bentworth, on the line from Basingstoke to Alton. He adds that the Lovers' Leap was probably at Hengistbury Head, which is fifty miles from Preston Candover, since no lovers, however suidical, could fling them-

selves into the sea between Chichester Harbour and the mouth
of the Beaulieu River with anything worse than a rather muddy
splash; and that manifestly Catsmeat said it was fifty miles, not
fifteen, to the Lovers' Leap, and that Bertie misheard him.

Reluctant as I am to question the opinion of so eminent a
critic as Howarth, I cannot accept this conclusion. I think the
extent to which a critic is justified in disregarding the text in
order to suit his theories has its limits. And when the critic has
to reject Catsmeat's clear statements that Deverill Hall was
twenty miles from Basingstoke, and that the Lovers' Leap was
fifteen miles from Deverill Hall, I think those limits have been
reached.

I do not believe that the evidence of the Lovers' Leap throws
any light on the location of Deverill Hall, because I do not think
we can assume that the Lovers' Leap was necessarily on the sea.
An inland craig, or even a quarry, would fit Catsmeat's description just as well. Nor do I believe that it can have been at
Hengistbury Head, which is a gentle mound of sand only just
over 100 feet high, and about 200 yards inland from the sea,
with nothing like a precipitous cliff anywhere. There is no cliff
on the coast to tempt the most star-crossed lover to suicidal
leaps anywhere between Seaford Head in Sussex and Standfast
Point in Dorset, both of which are much more than fifty miles,
let alone fifteen, from any conceivable location for Deverill Hall.

Turning to the railways, I would eliminate the G.W.R.
line from Basingstoke to Reading, not because it is in the
wrong direction for Lovers' Leaps, but because it is not a branch
line at all: it is an important through link for traffic between
Liverpool and Manchester in the north and Southampton and
Bournemouth in the south.

As regards the yell, of course Catsmeat (or Gertrude) was
exaggerating when he (or she) said it could have been heard in
Basingstoke. Even Bertie put it no higher than to say that Catsmeat 'hazarded the opinion' that the yell could be heard there.[15]
As a golfer, the critic Howarth ought to know that even the
most stentorian 'Fore' cannot be heard for more than about 300
yards, under the most favourable conditions of wind and
weather. So if he rejects Catsmeat's statement about the
distance, but accepts his statement that the yell could be heard

in Basingstoke, to what conclusion does his argument lead? It leads to the conclusion that Deverill Hall must have been within a quarter of a mile of the centre of Basingstoke. Basingstoke, no doubt, was not so big or so beastly then as it is now: but it seems improbable that there can ever have been a village with picturesque cottages and its own separate post office, police station and railway station so close to it.

No – what Gertrude must have told Catsmeat was that the yell *'sounded as though* it could have been heard in Basingstoke'. There is no evidence whatever that it actually was so heard. So there is no need to reject Catsmeat's statement that Deverill Hall was about twenty miles from Basingstoke; and so it cannot have been on the branch line from Basingstoke to Alton.

Where was it then? At first sight it is tempting to suggest that it was on the old single-track G.W.R. line from Didcot to Southampton (the 'Child of Sorrow' as it used to be called), which merged with the L.S.W.R. main line about two miles south of Winchester. If it was, Bertie would have had to change into a slow train at Basingstoke as far as Whitchurch. At Whitchurch he would have had to change not merely trains but also stations, and walk a mile from the L.S.W.R. station north of the town to the G.W.R. station at its south-west edge. This, one feels, may well have prompted his crack that 'once you're on the branch line, it's quicker to walk'. The G.W.R. line can properly be called a branch line, because it was never used as a through link from north to south or vice versa. It is true that, so far as Bertie's journey was concerned, the branch line would have started at Whitchurch and not at Basingstoke. But, with a little good will, I think this difficulty can be overcome. For Bertie did change into a slower train at Basingstoke (he says so very clearly), and the line from Basingstoke to Whitchurch, though actually the L.S.W.R. main line, must have seemed to him like a branch. There are, however, two fatal objections to this theory. First, no part of the Hampshire section of the G.W.R. line is more than eighteen miles from Basingstoke as the crow flies, and most of it is very much less. The only part which is anywhere near eighteen miles from Basingstoke is the part near Winchester; and if Deverill Hall was there, it would have been simpler to catch an express train to Winchester. Secondly, Bertie does not

mention having to change trains, let alone stations, on his journey to Wimbledon by the milk train; and there was no way in
which the milk train could have passed from the G.W.R. to the
L.S.W.R. system at Whitchurch. The stations were a mile apart,
and there was no loop line connecting them, as there is (or was),
for instance, at Peterborough or at Crianlarich in Perthshire.

For the first of the above reasons, we can also eliminate the
line from Alton to Winchester through Alresford and Itchen
Abbas; no part of it (except the extreme west end) is anywhere
near twenty miles from Basingstoke. So we are left with the line
from Alton to Fareham, with Meonstoke (exactly twenty miles
from Basingstoke) as the most likely place. I think that the critic
Howarth dismisses this rather too hastily on the ground that
no one would have approached King's Deverill through
Basingstoke when he could have caught a through train to Alton.
I think it is significant that Catsmeat, who as we have seen
arrived by train, did not complain about the slowness of the
branch line. He evidently caught a fast train from Waterloo to
Alton, after which four more stations (or about fourteen miles)
on the branch line would have brought him to Meonstoke/King's
Deverill. I would agree with Howarth that no ordinary man in
his senses would approach Meonstoke via Basingstoke. But Bertie was not an ordinary man, he was a chump: and just consider
what a time he had had in the last twelve hours, and you will
agree that he must have been in an overwrought state – just the
sort of state in which people get into the wrong train. He had to
stay awake for the first part of the night, in order not to miss the
2.54 a.m. milk train. That train crawled to Wimbledon, taking
nearly five hours on its journey. Bertie then had to hide in a bush
in the garden at The Larches, Wimbledon Common, waiting for
an opportunity to intercept Gussie's letter.[16] He then had to hide
behind a sofa, because his retreat was cut off by a gardener
wearing an M.C.C. cap.[17] He then had that painful scene with
Madeline Bassett, in the course of which she told him the plot
of *Mervyn Keene, Clubman*.[18] He then had to decline the solid
girl's invitation to breakfast, though he needed it sorely. And
finally he had the mortification of seeing Catsmeat whizz past
him in the drive and vanish over the skyline in Bertie's own
car.[19] No wonder he got into the wrong train.

But, you will object, he was already beginning to look like something the cat found in Tutankhamen's tomb,[20] and surely the booking clerk, the ticket inspectors, the guards and the porters along his route would have taken pity on him and seen to it that he got into the right train. Not a bit of it, for the old L.S.W.R. was notoriously reticent about the destinations of its trains. In *Three Men in a Boat* (chapter 5, sub-title: 'Innocence of South Western officials concerning such worldly things as trains'), Harris and Jerome were reduced to asking the engine-driver if he was going to Kingston, and even he didn't know. And this was at Waterloo, the London terminus and head-quarters of the line. What can they have known or cared about Hampshire branch lines at Wimbledon or Surbiton, where the only passenger traffic is suburban commuter traffic? Besides, Bertie may have told the booking clerk in so many words that he wanted to go via Basingstoke. He knew (because Esmond[21] and Catsmeat[22] both told him so) that the nearest decent cinema to King's Deverill was at Basingstoke. He may well have thought that Basingstoke was the nearest railway junction, too. It was probably dark when he drove through Alton on that spring evening when he first arrived; and even if it was light, how could he know that King's Deverill was best approached via Alton? There is no evidence that Bertie knew anything about the geography of the L.S.W.R. His journeys from King's Deverill to Wimbledon and back are his only recorded journeys on that system. So there are no rational grounds for eliminating Meonstoke as the most likely location for Deverill Hall.

PART 2. THE GOLF STORIES

11. THE DOMICILE OF AGNES FLACK

I. THE GOLF STORIES

Agnes Flack appears in five of Wodehouse's golf stories. He describes her as 'a dynamic and interesting personality',[1] thereby giving the reader a nudge (and himself a pat on the back) which would perhaps be unbecoming in the case of a younger author.

With the exception of No. 11 (*The Coming of Gowf*), which is a historical fantasy set in the mythical Kingdom of Oom, and which is so unlike the rest of the stories that it need not be further considered here, all the golf stories in *The Golf Omnibus* are set either in England or the United States. With three exceptions, they are all told in the first person by the Oldest Member. The three exceptions are No. 1, which is told by an unnamed narrator who fades out on the first page; No. 21, which is told by Mr Mulliner, the fisherman in the bar parlour of the Anglers' Rest; and No. 31, which is told in the third person. Agnes Flack is first introduced in No. 21, and makes her last bow in No. 31, so these two stories will have to be examined in greater detail below. The problem of this essay is, was she English or American? Or, to put it more technically, what was her domicile? I avoid the term nationality, because in British and American law a person can have dual nationality, but can only have one domicile at any one time.

II. THE OLDEST MEMBER

All but three of the stories are told by the Oldest Member, who moralises to his heart's content on golf, love, women and life in general. Sometimes he plays an active part in the stories which he tells; sometimes he is just a device, a voice which fades out soon after the story begins, and he reports dialogue which he could not have overheard, and describes scenes which he could not have witnessed. Still, it is possible to build up a character sketch of his appearance and personality. He was an old man with white hair,[2] white eyebrows[3] and white whiskers.[4] He was a bachelor[5] and had reached the age when he was no longer expected to dance.[6] Just how old was he? He must have been in his 70s, because he was up at the University with Joseph Poskitt,[7] one of the Wrecking Crew (of whom more anon), all four of whom were septuagenarians.[8] Yet he had not retired from business, because on one occasion he was away from home for many weeks on a protracted business tour.[9] He occasionally gave a golf lesson,[10] sometimes accompanied a younger man on a round,[11] and often refereed a match.[12] He often infested the seventh tee on a fine afternoon.[13] But he was usually to be found in his favourite chair[14] on the terrace outside the club house overlooking the ninth green.[15] Besides being a compulsive narrator, he was also a sympathetic listener, and most of the local young men, and some of the young women, came to him for advice on the problems which affected their golf or their love lives.

Had Wodehouse planned his golf stories as a series, instead of writing them as pot-boilers in the intervals between more important work, he might have had some fun in distinguishing between the appearance and personality of the English and the American Oldest Member. But he does not do this: and the preceding analysis is equally applicable to both. The critic Howarth has even suggested that the English and the American Oldest Members are one and the same person, partly from the lack of any distinguishing characteristics, and partly because, in the prologue to No. 26 (which is clearly set in the United States) the Oldest Member reveals that he is familiar with the story of Rollo Podmarsh, the hero of No.17, which is probably set in England. He deduces from this that the same Oldest Member told Nos. 17 and 26. But there is no need to adopt this rather improbable hypothesis, for the American narrator of No. 26 could easily have heard the story of No. 17 from one of his English friends, perhaps from his English opposite number.

It is true that one of the stories which is quite clearly set in the United States (No. 9) is told (as a reminiscence of his far-distant youth) by the English Oldest Member, who had just come down from Cambridge and secured the job of private and confidential secretary to an American multi-millionaire in Chicago.[16] On learning that his employer wanted to take up golf, he recommended as coach a Scottish professional named Sandy McHoots, who won the British and American Opens in the previous year.[17] Yet fifty years later, when the Oldest Member is narrating contemporary events, this same Sandy McHoots is still the Open Champion.[18] Rarely can a professional golfer have had a longer reign.

There are some serious discrepancies affecting the English Oldest Member. In one story he had, as stated above, just come down from Cambridge; in another he was up at the University with Joseph Poskitt (one of the Wrecking Crew) who got a blue at Oxford for throwing the hammer.[19] Moreover, as Howarth points out, the narrator of No. 7 (which is set in Marvis Bay) is clearly different from the Oldest Member who narrated other stories set in England. The Marvis Bay Oldest Member had not played golf since the rubber-cored ball superseded the old dignified gutty;[20] the other played two rounds in the same afternoon.[21] The Marvis Bay Oldest Member was a close student of the works of Marcus Aurelius, and thought he was a golfer, and a bad golfer at that;[22] the other never quoted Marcus Aurelius, and was convinced that the later Roman Emperors never played golf.[23] There is another story set in Marvis Bay (No. 12), but the comments of the Oldest Member who narrates it do not suggest that he was ever more than a casual visitor to that course.

There is nothing else for it: we must postulate at least three English Oldest Members; one at Marvis Bay, one old Oxonian and one old Cantab., and one American one.

Some critics have suggested that the Oldest Member must have been a Mulliner, and may even have been *the* Mr Mulliner, because their methods of telling their stories are remarkably alike. But this superficial similarity disappears on closer analysis.

(i) In most of the golf stories the Oldest Member is a character as well as a narrator – he gives sympathy or advice to the young, gives a golf lesson, referees a match, or even plays a round or two. Only in Nos. 2, 3, 5, 10, 13, 14, 17, 20, 23 and 26 (ten stories out of twenty-seven) is he a narrator pure and simple. Mr Mulliner on the other hand takes no part at all as a character in any of his 41 stories except Nos. 8, 10 and 40 – and in the first two of these he appears as a very shadowy character for less than a page.

(ii) In three stories (Nos. 3, 7 and 28) the Oldest Member is so keen to get off the mark that he does not even wait for an audience, but tells the story apparently as a soliloquy. Mr Mulliner never does such a thing. It is true that he appears to do so in Nos. 17 and 18, but this is probably an illusion. These are the second and third of three consecutive stories about Roberta Wickham, told after he had been away on a visit to her mother's home at Skeldings Hall. They are evidently meant to be told at one sitting, so that the audience assembled for No. 16 is meant to be there also for Nos. 17 and 18.

(iii) When we come to the content of the stories, the difference is even more marked. All the Mulliner stories are 'screwy' stories – in various degrees, incredible. That is why they have to be told by a fisherman, whose veracity (as Wodehouse says in the Preface to *The World of Mr Mulliner*) would be automatically suspect. The only screwy golf stories are No. 21, told by Mr Mulliner, and Nos. 11 and 31, told in the third person. No. 21 is screwy because John Gooch and Frederick Pilcher each tries to lose the golf match, since the penalty of victory is having to marry Agnes Flack. Such a thing would have been anathema to any of the Oldest Members, to all of whom golf was as much a religion as a game: they would have been horrified by such an attitude, and could not possibly have told such a story.

III. England or America?

Some of the stories are set quite clearly in England; others equally clearly in the United States. Sometimes the venue is not stated, and the author seems to go out of his way to leave it doubtful, for example by having his characters visit 'the metropolis' (and not London or New York). Yet in spite of this he does leave clues for the discerning critic to pick up. The difficulty is to evaluate them correctly, especially when (as sometimes happens) they point in different directions. We start with the hypothesis that place names are stronger evidence than the names of characters, since places cannot move (though they can be duplicated), while people can move from one country to the other. Thus, if a story with an obviously English setting takes place at Woodhaven (No. 3), it is reasonable to suppose that another story taking place at Woodhaven (No. 8) is also set in England. We know from a Bertie Wooster story[24] that Marvis Bay is in Dorset; therefore the two stories taking place there (Nos. 7 and 12) must presumably be set in England. On the other hand, if Peter Willard (the keenest but the worst golfer in the club) is mentioned in four English stories (Nos. 3, 15, 16 and 20), we cannot safely infer from his appearance in another story (No. 27) that it too is set in England, if there are indications to the contrary.

Other clues are perhaps more subtle. If a character takes a train to Scotland (No. 10), or drives seventy miles in the general direction of Scotland (No. 30), surely that indicates an English setting. If a golfer takes a tennis lesson to please his lady love and is informed by the pro. that there is no flag, because it is not the Fourth of July (No. 25), surely the setting must be American. The same is true if a character has to attend a luncheon in Washington with the President of the United States (No. 26). References to pounds or shillings, to the Crimean War, the Cornish Riviera Express, Wormwood Scrubs or the Stock Exchange suggest an English setting, at least if there are no counter indications; references to dollars, Sing Sing or Wall Street suggest an American one.

No deductions can safely be drawn from the descriptions of the various holes on the courses where the matches take place, partly because the Oldest Member often says that the course has been remodelled or replanned since the story he is narrating, and partly because nearly all the courses in both countries have two features in common: the terrace outside the club house overlooks the ninth green;[25] and the second hole is the lake hole, a par three.[26]

Weighing all these clues as carefully as I can, I venture to place Nos. 1, 9, 13, 14, 25, 26, 27, 29 and 31 of the stories in the United States, and Nos. 2, 3, 4, 5, 6, 7, 8, 10, 12, 21, 23 and 30 in England. There remain for consideration Nos. 15, 16, 17, 18, 19, 20, 22, 24 and 28. (No. 11, the historical fantasy, is, as previously stated, not considered here.)

(i) In No. 15, a member of the Wrecking Crew drove into Chester Meredith and caused him to foozle just when he was about to lower the record for his home course. The Wrecking Crew was a 'quartette of spavined septuagenarians whose pride it was that they never let anyone through',[27] even when they were playing a fourball foursome. Their nicknames were the First Grave Digger, the Man with the Hoe, Old Father Time, and Consul, the Almost Human. The only clue to the setting of No. 15 is that when the Oldest Member tries to console Chester Meredith for having lost his girl by reminding him that 'there is always golf', he encourages him to hope that he could win the Amateur Championship, the Open, the American Amateur and the American Open. The order in which these championships are mentioned, plus the fact that no 'British' precedes the first two, is some indication that the story is set in England.

(ii) In No. 22 Joseph Poskitt, the star performer of the Wrecking Crew, entered for the President's Cup. The only indications of the setting are (a) that he was a member of the Wrecking Crew, who are also mentioned in No. 30, a story clearly set in England; (b) that the Oldest Member was unable to witness the contest for the President's Cup because business in London claimed him; and (c) that the hero, Wilmot Byng, ate a lunch consisting of steak and kidney pudding, treacle tart and a spot of Stilton. These indications surely point to an English setting. But there is a mystery about the President's Cup. In No. 15 it was twice won by Chester Meredith, a very fine golfer; but in No. 22 it was open only to members with a handicap not lower than twenty-four, and ranked somewhere between the Grandmothers' Umbrella and the Children's All-Day Sucker, open to boys and girls under seven. These three trophies were also offered for competition in No. 27, which is definitely set in the United States.

(iii) The only clue to the setting of No. 16 is that the hero, Wallace Chesney, bought a suit of second-hand plus fours (made to measure for Sandy McHoots, the British Open Champion, who lived in Scotland) from a junk shop 'in the City' run by the Cohen Brothers. In No. 13 of the Mulliner stories, there is a shop in Covent Garden run by the Cohen Brothers which sells just the same sort of junk. So, although Covent Garden is not technically in the City, it looks as though the setting is English. In No. 17, Rollo Podmarsh caught sight of Wallace Chesney's plus fours gleaming down in the valley by the second hole, and thought they looked lovely. So the setting of No. 17 is presumably English too. On the other hand, in the prologue to No. 26, which is clearly set in the United States, the American Oldest Member reveals that he knows the story of Rollo Podmarsh: but, as we have seen, it does not follow that Nos. 17 and 26 were told by the same person, nor that they took place in the same country.

(iv) Nos. 18, 19, 20 and 28 are all stories about William Bates, Jane Packard and Rodney Spelvin. The only firm and reliable clues to the setting are that in No. 28 there is a mention of *The Tatler* and of Wormwood Scrubbs. But the characters all seem essentially English, and on that ground also I incline to place these stories in England. It is true that in Nos. 18 and 20 a course called Squashy Hollow (which sounds American) is mentioned: but Squashy Hollow is a most unreliable guide. First, there are two American Squashy Hollows – one 5 miles away from Goldenville, Long Island (No. 14), and one near Paradise Valley (No. 31), which must be a different course, because the 'soft mountain breezes' were a feature of the environment, and there are no mountains in Long Island. There is also a course called Squashy Hollow in England: it is mentioned in No. 7 of the Mulliner stories. Lastly, to add to the confusion, there is an English course called Squashy Heath which is mentioned in No. 30 of the golf stories.

(v) In No. 24, the only clue pointing to an English setting is the Oldest Member's statement that he once caught a fish off Brighton pier. The only clue pointing to an American setting is that three very minor characters, Perkins, Alfred Jukes and Wilberforce Bream reappear (again as very minor characters) in two other stories (Nos. 13 and 27) which are clearly set in the United States.

I conclude that of the nine stories listed above whose setting is doubtful, Nos. 15, 16, 17, 18, 19, 20, 22 and 28 are set in England, and that there is insufficient evidence in No. 24 for even an intelligent guess.

IV. AGNES FLACK

We are now in a position to tackle the elusive problem of Agnes Flack's domicile. She was a fine, large, handsome girl[28] who stood five feet ten inches tall in her stockings[29] and weighed 160 lbs.,[30] or 11 stone,[31] and was all muscle.[32] She had shoulders and forearms which would have excited the envious admiration of one of those muscular women of the music-halls who good-naturedly allow six brothers, three sisters and a cousin by marriage to pile themselves on her collar-bone while the orchestra plays a long-drawn chord. Her eye resembled the eye of one of the more imperious queens of history.[33] She sometimes had the appearance of one who is about to play Boadicea in a pageant.[34] Built rather on the lines of the village blacksmith, she had the shoulders of an all-in wrestler, the breezy self-confidence of a sergeant-major and a voice like a toastmaster's.[35] Her penetrating voice sounded like the down express letting off steam at a level crossing.[36] When she laughed, strong men clutched at their temples to keep the tops of their heads from breaking loose.[37] Her laughter was like a steam riveter at work[38] or a train going through a tunnel.[39] When Sidney McMurdo proposed to her for the first time – on the sixth green – distant rumblings of her mirth were plainly heard in the club-house locker-room, causing two men who were afraid of thunderstorms to cancel their match.[40] Although she was a scratch golfer[41] and the undisputed female champion of the club,[42] having won the Ladies' Vase twice in successive years,[43] she once wrote a novel[44] which her fiancé Sidney McMurdo told her was a lot of prune juice and should be burnt without delay.[45] Evidently, Honoria Glossop could have taken her correspondence course.

Sidney McMurdo weighed 211 lbs.,[46] or 15 stone,[47] and was all muscle too.[48] He looked like the worthy descendant of a long line of heavy-weight gorillas.[49] He had once been a semi-finalist in the Amateur Championship;[50] but for reasons which (as we

shall see) are not hard to guess, his game seems subsequently to
have gone to pieces, because his handicap rose to 15, and Agnes
had to take him in hand and get him back to plus one.[51] His
habit when in form of always driving 250 yards from the tee
fascinated Agnes,[52] who could never manage more than 240
yards herself;[53] while Sidney in his turn was enthralled by Agnes's
short game, which was exceptionally accurate.[54]

Sidney loved Agnes with an ox-like devotion;[55] but he had to
propose to her twelve times before she accepted him.[56] However,
she broke off the engagement four times because he incurred her
displeasure for some reason, and each time got engaged to
someone else, to Sidney's fury.[57] In the last of the stories (No.
31), she is reunited to Sidney; but with her history of emotional
instability, who can tell how long that engagement lasted?

Agnes Flack appears in five stories, Nos. 21, 26, 29, 30 and 31.
The first of these is told by Mr Mulliner, who says that she was
the daughter of a distant cousin of his – one of the Devonshire
Mulliners who married a man named Flack. He tells the two
young men in chessboard knickerbockers at the Anglers' Rest
that she was always playing in tournaments and competitions,
and wonders whether they have run across her. So, in this story
Agnes was undoubtedly English, because the two young men
were clearly English, since the appearance of an American in the
Anglers' Rest was a rare event, a matter for special comment
and remark.[58]

However, in No. 26 it appears that Agnes is the only niece of
Josiah Flack, one of the richest men in America. And Agnes says
to the fortune-hunting Captain Fosdyke 'You're English, aren't
you?' This does not actually prove that she has now settled in
the United States; but since the story is undoubtedly set there
(because Captain Fosdyke has a lunch engagement in Washington with President Truman), it seems more than likely that she
has.

No. 29 is also set in the United States, because (in addition to
some faint indications to that effect – references to the Empire
State Building and the Grand Canyon of Arizona) Sidney
McMurdo has become a second vice-president of the Jersey City
and All Points West Mutual and Co-operative Life and Accident
Insurance Company.

But No. 30 is in all probability set in England. The evidence for this is as follows:

(i) John Rockett, who was twice British Amateur Champion and three times runner-up in the Open, calls his five children Sandwich, Hoylake, St Andrew, Troon and Prestwick after the courses on which he had won renown.

(ii) Eight English publishing firms are mentioned, and no American ones.

(iii) Harold Pickering drives about seventy miles in the general direction of Scotland – surely an unlikely description of any motor journey undertaken in the United States.

However, No. 31 is firmly set in the United States, because we are distinctly told that the hero, Cyril Grooly, was junior partner in a New York firm of publishers; and the currency is dollars.

So it seems that in No. 21 Agnes Flack is domiciled in England, that in Nos. 26 and 29 she is domiciled in one of the United States, that in No. 30 she has resumed her English domicile of origin, and that in No. 31 she has reacquired an American domicile of choice. Evidently, she changed her domicile as frequently as she changed her fiancés – and each time she changed her domicile, the faithful Sidney McMurdo changed his too. It is strange that neither of them gave their names to a leading case in the Conflict of Laws.

PART 3. BLANDINGS CASTLE

12. THE CHRONOLOGY OF THE BLANDINGS SAGA

I THE ORDER OF THE STORIES

Wodehouse was aware that the Blandings Castle Saga contains a number of discrepancies, for in *Pigs Have Wings* he is concerned to rebut the slur that he has just committed one.

Carpers and cavillers [he says] of whom there are far too many around these days, will interrupt at this point with a derisive 'Hoy cocky! Aren't you forgetting something?' thinking that they have caught the historian out in one of those blunders which historians sometimes make. But the historian has made no blunder.[1]

Maybe he has not in this particular instance. But still, the Saga does contain a mass of irreconcilable statements which render the task of the critic an unenviable one. Nowhere is the confusion more rife than in the matter of chronology.

Our first task is to establish the order of the stories. Here is a tentative list, with the year of first publication in brackets:

Pre-porcine period
  (i) *Something Fresh* (1915)
  (ii) *Leave it to Psmith* (1923)
  (iii) 'The Custody of the Pumpkin', in *Blandings Castle* (1935)
  (iv) 'Lord Emsworth and the Girl Friend', in *Blandings Castle* (1935)
  (v) 'Lord Emsworth Acts for the Best', in *Blandings Castle* (1935)

Porcine Period
  (vi) 'Pig-hoo-o-o-o-ey!' in *Blandings Castle* (1935)
  (vii) 'Company for Gertrude', in *Blandings Castle* (1935)
  (viii) 'The Go-Getter', in *Blandings Castle* (1935)

(ix) 'The Crime Wave at Blandings', in *Lord Emsworth and Others* (1937)

(x) *Summer Lightning* (1929)

(xi) *Heavy Weather* (1933)

(xii) *Uncle Fred in the Springtime* (1939)

(xiii) *Full Moon* (1947)

(xiv) *Pigs Have Wings* (1952)

(xv) *Service with a Smile* (1962)

(xvi) *Galahad at Blandings* (1965)

(xvii) 'Birth of a Salesman', in *Nothing Serious* (1950)

(xviii) *A Pelican at Blandings* (1969)

(xix) *Sunset at Blandings* (1977)

There is also 'Sticky Wicket at Blandings', a short story in *Plum Pie* (1966), but it is impossible even to guess at its place in the sequence, save to remark that, since Lady Constance Keeble is the chatelaine of Blandings, and Freddie Threepwood has married Niagara ('Aggie') Donaldson, it must come somewhere between (iii) and (xvi).

The reasons for this tentative order are as follows:

(i) *Something Fresh* is the first in the series: Wodehouse says so twice,[2] and the point is not disputed. It takes place in the spring.[3]

(ii) *Leave it to Psmith* is the second in the series.[4] It takes place in the first week in July.[5] An interval of at least two and a quarter years must have elapsed since *Something Fresh*, because Lady Constance Keeble has succeeded Lady Ann Warblington as chatelaine of Blandings, and she has been chatelaine for at least eighteen months.[6] The County Ball takes place at Shiffey at the end of the story.[7]

(iii) The next long novels are the two companion ones, *Summer Lightning* and *Heavy Weather*, in each of which Lord Emsworth's nephew Ronnie Fish is engaged to Sue Brown, the chorus girl, and Empress of Blandings has won her first silver medal at the Shropshire Agricultural Show and is striving to repeat the performance.[8] The Show does not take place until soon after August 14th, the date on which Lord Emsworth as trustee signs the cheque in favour of Ronnie.[9] These two stories take place in the last half of July[10] and the first half of August.[11]

They are separated by an interval of only a few days,[12] but in that short time an event of momentous importance to the chronologer occurs: Lord Emsworth celebrates his sixtieth birthday. (He was in his sixtieth year in *Summer Lightning*[13] and aged sixty in *Heavy Weather*.[14]) *Summer Lightning* must take place two years after *Leave it to Psmith*, because we are told that 'that flower-pot incident' occurred 'two years ago'.[15] In *Summer Lightning* Ronnie Fish steals the Empress, which is eventually discovered in Baxter's caravan; but Lord Emsworth is convinced that Baxter was the thief, and that he was a minion in the pay of Sir Gregory Parsloe-Parsloe of Matchingham Hall.[16]

(iv) Wodehouse says that the six short stories in *Blandings Castle* come after *Leave it to Psmith* and before *Summer Lightning*.[17] The difficulty is to fit them into that interval of two years. The first of the six is evidently 'The Custody of the Pumpkin'. In this story Freddie Threepwood (Lord Emsworth's younger son) marries Niagara ('Aggie') Donaldson, the only daughter of the American proprietor of Donaldson's Dog Biscuits Inc.; and Lord Emsworth's pumpkin wins first prize at the Shrewsbury Agricultural Show, breaking a three-year run of successes by his neighbour Sir Gregory Parsloe-Parsloe. The actual month of this story is something of a mystery. Pumpkins ripen in September; but Lord Emsworth narrowly escapes arrest for picking tulips in Kensington Gardens, and tulips are in bloom in April and May.

(v) 'Lord Emsworth and the Girl Friend' is dated very precisely on August Bank Holiday (i.e. the first Monday in August), when the Blandings Parva school treat was held in the grounds of Blandings Castle, much to Lord Emsworth's disgust. It is evidently later than 'The Custody of the Pumpkin', because there is a reference to the flouting and resignation of Angus McAllister 'at the time when they were grooming for the Agricultural Show that pumpkin which subsequently romped home so gallant a winner'. And it evidently belongs to the pre-porcine period, because when anarchy broke out in the tea tent, and the curate was doing his best to form a provisional government consisting of himself and the two school-teachers, and a rock-cake removed Lord Emsworth's top hat, he sought solace not at the Empress's sty, but in a cowshed.

(vi) 'Lord Emsworth Acts for the Best' comes next, for Freddie has been married for eight months.

(vii) 'Pig-hoo-o-o-o-ey!' is the first of the stories in the porcine period. The Empress wins her first silver medal in the Fat Pigs class at the eighty-seventh annual Shropshire Agricultural Show, which took place that year on July 30th or 31st.

(viii) 'Company for Gertrude' and 'The Go-Getter' (in that order) appear to be the next two stories of the six. They both take place in the summer, because in the former Lord Emsworth has a bathe in the lake before breakfast, and in the latter the curtains of the amber drawing-room are not drawn after dinner.

(ix) We must resist the temptation to fit some of these short stories into the gap between *Something Fresh* and *Leave it to Psmith*. As we have seen, Wodehouse himself says that they come between *Leave it to Psmith* and *Summer Lightning*. Although Wodehouse's statements in his Prefaces are not always reliable, as we shall see when we come to the problem of where Market Blandings is, this one is corroborated. For Freddie is still unmarried throughout *Leave it to Psmith*, but marries Niagara ('Aggie') Donaldson in 'The Custody of the Pumpkin', which must be the first of the six short stories, since all the others refer back to it.

(x) 'The Crime Wave at Blandings' must also be fitted into this two-year interval between *Leave it to Psmith* and *Summer Lightning*. Baxter was dismissed as Lord Emsworth's secretary at the end of *Leave it to Psmith*. In 'The Crime Wave at Blandings', Lady Constance Keeble re-engages him as tutor to Lord Emsworth's grandson George, the younger son of Viscount Bosham, in the middle of the summer holidays,[18] i.e. presumably in middle or late August. The story belongs to the porcine period, because Lord Emsworth is reading Whiffle on *The Care of the Pig*.[19] It comes after *Leave it to Psmith* and before *Summer Lightning*, because Lord Emsworth has it in for Baxter for throwing flower pots into his lordship's bedroom in the small hours of the morning,[20] but not for stealing the pig and hiding it in Baxter's caravan.

(xi) Despite its unsuitability as a month in which tulips and pumpkins are both at their best, I incline to place 'The Custody of the Pumpkin' in late July, i.e. about three weeks after the end of *Leave it to Psmith*; 'Lord Emsworth and the Girl Friend' on August Bank Holiday, a few days later; 'Lord Emsworth Acts for the Best' eight months later, in late March or early April; 'Pig-hoo-o-o-o-ey!' in late July of the same year; 'Company for Gertrude' and 'The Go-Getter' in early August; and 'The Crime Wave at Blandings' in the middle or late August of the same year.

(xii) *Summer Lightning* and *Heavy Weather* therefore took place in the following summer (late July and early August). The odious detective Percy Pilbeam is at Blandings in both these books. *Uncle Fred in the Springtime* takes place in the following April, since the month is stated and Pilbeam was at the Castle 'last summer'.[21] In this story the Empress has won her second silver medal.[22]

(xiii) *Full Moon* takes place in the summer[23] of the same year, before the Agricultural Show, because the Empress has won only two successive silver medals.[24] The month is not stated specifically, but is probably late June or early July, because Beach the butler brings a bowl of strawberries in for tea.[25] It is true that we cannot safely deduce the month at Blandings from the mention of particular flowers, fruit or vegetables, because in that earthly Paradise they all seem to bloom out of season. For instance, wallflowers were in bloom at Blandings in the second half of July;[26] and we have already commented on the fact that pumpkins were ripening at Blandings while tulips were in bloom in Kensington Gardens. These phenomena were due not so much to Angus McAllister's skill as to some magic property in the soil, since even in the cottage gardens at Blandings Parva wallflowers were in bloom on August Bank Holiday.[27] However, there is corroborative evidence that *Full Moon* took place in June: it is two weeks before the County Ball,[28] and as we have seen, this event takes place at the end of the first week in July. In this story Lord Emsworth's niece Veronica Wedge becomes engaged to the American millionaire Tipton Plimsoll.[29]

(xiv) *Pigs Have Wings* takes place a month or two later, probably in August, because at the end of the story the Empress wins her third successive silver medal. She defeats an outsider from Kent which Sir Gregory Parsloe-Parsloe has cunningly imported, contrary to all the conventions and traditions (but not to the written rules) governing the Shropshire Agricultural Show.[30]

(xv) The next story is *Service with a Smile*. It takes place in high summer, because the boys of the Church Lads Brigade, camped out in the grounds of Blandings Castle, are always bathing in the lake. The actual month is not stated, but is probably July, because the Empress has only won three successive silver medals,[31] and Lord Emsworth is sixty-one[32] (he was, as we have seen, sixty when the Empress won her second medal, soon after the end of *Heavy Weather*): therefore the date must be before Lord Emsworth's birthday in early August. At the end of this story Lady Constance Keeble becomes engaged to Jimmy (alias Johnny[33]) Schoonmaker,[34] an American friend of Galahad and of Lord Ickenham, and the father of that Myra Schoonmaker[35] whom Sue Brown impersonated in *Summer Lightning*.

(xvi) *Galahad at Blandings* comes next. It begins in the middle of August.[36] The Empress has won three silver medals,[37] but although the Agricultural Show must be imminent, there is no suggestion that she is expected to win a fourth. (I shall try to unravel this mystery in a later essay.) At the beginning of the story, Lord Emsworth is (most improbably) staying at the Plaza Hotel, New York, in order to attend Lady Constance Keeble's wedding to Jimmy Schoonmaker.[38] Veronica Wedge is still engaged to Tipton Plimsoll.[39] The wedding is fixed for early September at Blandings, with the whole county at the reception.[40] But Tipton and Veronica think that a big society wedding is a lot of prune juice, and decide to elope and get married at a registrar's instead.[41] The story ends with them heading for the registrar's 'the day after tomorrow'.[42]

(xvii) The next story is 'Birth of a Salesman'. Something must have happened to upset Tipton's and Veronica's plans, for Lord Emsworth is staying with his son Freddie at the latter's home on Long Island, N.Y., to attend the wedding of 'one of his nieces' (presumably Veronica) to Tipton Plimsoll. Since they were mad keen to get married at the end of *Galahad at Blandings*, I see no reason to suppose that the wedding was postponed for more than a week or two. Another reason for not placing 'Birth of a Salesman' later is that Freddie has been working for Donaldson's

Dog Biscuits Inc. for three years (it should have been four, but let that pass).

(xviii) In *A Pelican at Blandings* Lord Emsworth and Hermione are no longer on speaking terms,[43] and Constance is married to James Schoonmaker and has been living with him in New York for 'a longish time'.[44] This suggests that the story took place about a year after *Galahad at Blandings*. It is high summer,[45] as it always is at Blandings (except in *Something Fresh* and *Uncle Fred in the Springtime*). Gladioli are in bloom,[46] which suggests that the month is August or September. But, as we have seen, it is never safe to deduce the month at Blandings from the mention of particular flowers, and (for reasons to be mentioned shortly) the most likely month is June or July.

(xix) The last story is *Sunset at Blandings*, on which Wodehouse was working when he died. It is unfinished and unrevised, so one must be cautious when dealing with the evidence it yields. It takes place in high summer, a week after the end of *A Pelican at Blandings*,[47] but before the beginning of August, because Dame Daphne Winkworth's school at Eastbourne has not yet broken up for the summer holidays.[48]

(xx) It will be seen that the star witness for the chronology of the stories in the porcine period is the Empress of Blandings. She wins her first silver medal at the Shropshire Agricultural Show in 'Pig-hoo-o-o-o-ey!'; repeats the performance next year, shortly after *Heavy Weather*; and wins her third and last medal in the following year, in *Pigs Have Wings*.

II. THE DURATION OF THE SAGA

As we have seen, there is an interval of at least two and a quarter years between *Something Fresh* and *Leave it to Psmith*; two years between *Leave it to Psmith* and *Summer Lightning*; one year between *Summer Lightning* and *Pigs have Wings*; another year between *Pigs Have Wings* and *Galahad at Blandings*; and nearly a year between *Galahad at Blandings* and *A Pelican at Blandings*. There is no direct evidence as to whether the interval between *Something Fresh* and *Leave it to Psmith* was longer than two and a quarter years. I am inclined to think that the interval was seven and a quarter years, for reasons which I shall give when we come to the dates of the stories.

It is true that, in *Something Fresh*, the head gardener at Blandings is a man named Thorne,[49] and there is no mention of Angus McAllister; and that in 'The Custody of the Pumpkin', Angus McAllister has served Lord Emsworth faithfully for ten years. But it by no means follows that the interval between those two stories was as long as ten years, for two reasons. First, we are not actually told that Angus McAllister has been head gardener for ten years. He may have started as a gardener's boy and worked up through under-gardener to head gardener. If so, he may well have been employed at Blandings Castle in *Something Fresh*, even though he is not mentioned by name. Secondly, we are told many times that Beach has been at Blandings for eighteen or nineteen years;[50] but these statements are obviously unreliable, because the length of his service must have increased as the Saga unfolds.

I conclude that the Saga lasted about twelve and a quarter years.

III. The Dates of the Stories

Our next task is to try and establish the dates when the stories took place. The evidence is very confusing.

(i) In *Something Fresh*, we are told that Lord Emsworth was at Eton in the 1860s.[51] If he went to Eton when he was thirteen and left when he was eighteen, he must have been born some time between 1847 and 1851 inclusive. But in the Preface to the 1969 edition of *Something Fresh*, Wodehouse withdrew this statement, remarking that while the ninth earl was not supposed to be in his first youth, he certainly did not intend to portray him as a centenarian.

(ii) In *Leave it to Psmith*, we are told that in the summer of 1874 Lord Emsworth heard his father's footsteps approaching the stable-loft in which he, a lad of fifteen, sat smoking his first cigar.[52] According to this statement, which is uncorroborated, Lord Emsworth must have been born in 1859. As we have seen, he attained the age of sixty in the short interval between *Summer Lightning* and *Heavy Weather*. If we accept this evidence, it means that those two stories should be dated in 1919, and *Leave it to Psmith* in 1917.

(iii) However, there is evidence that *Leave it to Psmith* must have taken place after 1919. First, Psmith reads *The Girls' Pet* for January 1919 in the waiting room of Miss Ada Clarkson's Employment Agency, and reflects that employment agencies, like dentists, prefer their literature of a matured vintage.[53] Secondly, Susan Simmons, the detective masquerading as a housemaid at Blandings, whose hobby it was to remember dates with precision, reminds Baxter that they had worked together before, from December 16th 1918 to January 12th 1919, when Baxter was secretary to Mr Horace Jevons, the American millionaire.[54] Thirdly, *Leave it to Psmith* took place in 'the only fine July that England had known in the last ten years'.[55] So the most likely date for *Leave it to Psmith* is 1921, when the summer (especially July) was exceptionally fine. This is a much more probable date than 1917, when of course there was a war on.

(iv) *Something Fresh* took place, as we have seen, at least two and a quarter years before *Leave it to Psmith*. I am inclined to think that it took place in the spring of 1914 – not later, for two reasons. First, if we date it later, there would have been a war on – and surely there were too many young men of military age on both sides of the green baize door for that to be credible. Secondly, *Something Fresh* was first published in America in 1914, and was probably written in late 1913 or early 1914: and I do not believe that Wodehouse ever imagined that the events he was writing about happened in the future.

(v) The Hon. Galahad Threepwood was four years younger than his brother Lord Emsworth.[56] He was educated at Eton[57] and Oxford.[58] In 1906 he attended a garden party at Buckingham Palace with a girl named Mabel,[59] which is surprising, because although he had some aristocratic friends, he also had some very disreputable ones – e.g. bookmakers, barmaids, skittle sharps and jellied eel sellers on racecourses.[60] In between his Oxford days and his attendance at the Buckingham Palace garden party, he painted London red in the 1890s with his aristocratic cronies of the old Pelican Club. In later life he used to tell stories of these adventures, and frequently dated them with precision, much to the delight of the conscientious chronologer. There was the story about Buffy Struggles in 1893, who was run over and killed by a hansom cab in Piccadilly because he gave up alcohol and started drinking tea;[61] the oft-told tale of how Galahad and Puffy Benger stole old Wivenhoe's pig the night of the Bachelors' Ball at Hammer's Easton in 1895, and put it in Plug Basham's bedroom;[62] the story of how Gregory Parsloe-Parsloe won £10 7s 6d from Galahad in 1895 with a doctored spinning top;[63] of how Parsloe stole Lord Burper's false teeth in 1896 and pawned them in a shop in the Edgware Road;[64] of how Parsloe and Galahad backed their dogs against rats for £100 a side in 1897, and Parsloe took Galahad's dog Towser aside just before the contest and gave him about six pounds of steak and onions, so that he gave a long yawn, rolled over and went to sleep;[65] of how Barmy Bellamy suffered from spells in 1897, just like Baxter did later;[66] of how old Freddie Potts in 1898 was saved from an exceedingly unpleasant attack of hedgehog poisoning because he lived almost entirely on Scotch whisky;[67] of how old Beefy Muspratt, with some assistance, smashed a billiard table in 1898;[68] of how Stiffy Vokes had to sneak about London in 1899 in a false beard and calling himself Orlando Maltravers, in the empty hope of baffling the bookies after a bad City and Suburban;[69] of how Jack Bellamy-Johnstone fell in love with a girl named Esmeralda Parkinson-Willoughby in 1899, and had her full name tattoed on his wishbone, and when the wounds had scarcely healed they quarrelled and he got engaged to another girl called May Todd ('so if he had only waited');[70] and of how his brother-in-law Major-General Sir Miles Fish, when a young subaltern, rode a bicycle down Piccadilly in sky-blue underclothing in 1897, and, returning to his rooms in the early morning of New Year's Day 1902, mistook the coal-scuttle for a mad dog and tried to shoot it with the fire-tongs.[71]

I hope I have said enough to establish Galahad in the reader's mind as a credible witness, and one who was fully alive to the importance of accurate chronology. I come now to his crucial evidence. Galahad was madly in love with a music hall singer named Dolly Henderson in 1896, 1897 and 1898.[72] To stop him marrying her, his father the eighth earl hauled him home to

Blandings[73] and then shipped him off to South Africa.[74] Galahad heard quite casually in a Johannesburg bar that she had married Captain Jack Cotterleigh of the Irish Guards.[75] This must have been in late 1898 or early 1899, for Galahad was back in London again in 1899, as is proved by his stories about Stiffy Vokes and Jack Bellamy-Johnstone. The Cotterleighs had a daughter, a chorus girl professionally known as Sue Brown, who became engaged to Lord Emsworth's nephew Ronnie Fish. Although she is rather vague about the dates, she tells Galahad in *Heavy Weather* that she had been engaged to Monty Bodkin two and a half or three years ago, when she was about seventeen.[76] So she must have been twenty at the time of *Summer Lightning* and *Heavy Weather*.

(vi) But, alas, there are some discrepancies.

(a) Ronnie's mother Lady Julia Fish was only a child in 1898, when Galahad was shipped off to South Africa.[77] She married the dashing young subaltern of 1897 and 1902 after he had become a stodgily respectable colonel.[78] And their son Ronnie was aged twenty-five at the time of *Summer Lightning*.[79] I do not know how long it takes for a dashing young subaltern to get promoted in peacetime through Captain and Major into a stodgily respectable Colonel: but I should think it must take at least eight years. If so, Ronnie could not have been born before 1911, and the date of *Summer Lightning* and *Heavy Weather* must be 1936 – an impossibly late date.

(b) In *Heavy Weather*, Lord Emsworth says that Galahad was shipped off to South Africa thirty years ago.[80] Perhaps we can discount this piece of evidence on the ground that the ninth earl was not the most reliable of witnesses. But Galahad himself says two years later in *Galahad at Blandings* that it was odd that he could still have that choked-up feeling after thirty years when he thought of Dolly Henderson.[81] This evidence, if we can believe it, would place *Summer Lightning* and *Heavy Weather* in 1926.

(c) In 1912 Beach was apparently employed, not by Lord Emsworth, but by old General Magnus, because Galahad wanted to consult Beach about 'that trouble in 1912'.[82] So if Beach had been at Blandings for eighteen years, *Summer Lightning* and *Heavy Weather* cannot have taken place before 1930.

(vii) It remains to consider some quite different evidence which

consists not in Threepwood family history but in topical allusions scattered through the stories. The weight of this evidence
is low indeed, and it leads in one case at least to a ludicrous
conclusion.

(a) In 'The Custody of the Pumpkin', Freddie's newly-acquired
father-in-law Mr Donaldson, of Donaldson's Dog Biscuits Inc.,
tells Lord Emsworth that he is not a rich man, having only ten
million dollars in the world, but that he is a firm believer in
President Roosevelt's New Deal, under which the American dog
is beginning to eat more biscuits. This would place that story in
1933 or later.

(b) In 'Pig-hoo-o-o-o-ey!', Lord Emsworth, lunching with
James Belford at the Senior Conservative Club, tells him that he
is worried because the Empress has declined all nourishment
just before the Agricultural Show; and James Belford tells Lord
Emsworth that there is a master call which will make any pig
start feeding again. He teaches it to Lord Emsworth, thereby
causing ninety-three Senior Conservatives, lunching in the vicin-
ity, to congeal into living statues of alarm and disapproval. But
when he returns to Blandings, Lord Emsworth characteristically
forgets what the second syllable of the master word is. He is
only reminded of it when he hears the housekeeper's gramo-
phone in the servants' hall playing a record called 'WHO stole
my heart away?' This was the hit tune of a musical comedy
called 'Sunny', which opened at the London Hippodrome on
October 7th 1926 with Binnie Hale in the name part. So the
story cannot, according to this evidence, have taken place earlier
than 1927.

(c) In 'Company for Gertrude', Freddie tells Rupert Bingham
that he could ingratiate himself with Stalin if he gave his mind
to it. It was not until about 1926 that it became known in the
west that Stalin had succeeded Lenin as the ruler of Russia.

(d) In 'Birth of a Salesman', Lord Emsworth, visiting America
for the wedding of one of his nieces (presumably Veronica
Wedge) to Tipton Plimsoll, is forced to stay with his son Freddie
at the latter's home in Long Island, because the British Government will not allow him enough foreign currency to stay in a
New York hotel. Since there was no foreign exchange control in
this country before the outbreak of war in 1939, this must be a

reference to that short period under the first post-war Labour Government when, at the behest of the trade unions (and before cheap package tours for the masses were invented), the holiday travel allowance was reduced to £25 per person per annum. This would place that story in 1948 or 1949 (it was published in 1950). Lord Emsworth had no such difficulty in the immediately preceding story (*Galahad at Blandings*) when he stayed at the Plaza Hotel, New York, in order to attend Lady Constance Keeble's wedding.[83] That story probably took place as long ago as 1925 (it is, as we have seen, two years after *Summer Lightning* and *Heavy Weather*). At the end of *Galahad at Blandings*, Tipton and Veronica were just about to get married. So, if this evidence from 'Birth of a Salesman' is to be believed, they must have remained an engaged couple for another twenty-three or twenty-four years. I submit with confidence that such evidence is quite unreliable, and that, like the thirteenth stroke of a clock, it throws doubt on all the other evidence of topical allusions assembled above.

But what are we to make of the rest of this conflicting evidence? Obviously, it is irreconcilable: some of it must be rejected. I think we must reject the evidence (consisting as it does of one unconfirmed statement by Wodehouse) that Lord Emsworth was born in 1859 and place the date of his birth in 1863. For, as we have seen, 1921 is a much more likely date for *Leave it to Psmith* than 1917. Lord Emsworth attained the age of sixty between the end of *Summer Lightning* and the beginning of *Heavy Weather*, so that those stories can be dated in 1923. We then have the following:

Pre-porcine period

Spring 1914	*Something Fresh*
Early July 1921	*Leave it to Psmith*
Late July 1921	'The Custody of the Pumpkin'
August 1921	'Lord Emsworth and the Girl Friend'
March 1922	'Lord Emsworth Acts for the Best'

Porcine period

Late July 1922	'Pig-hoo-o-o-o-ey!'
Early August 1922	'Company for Gertrude'
Early August 1922	'The Go-Getter'

Late August 1922	'The Crime Wave at Blandings'
Late July 1923	*Summer Lightning*
Early August 1923	*Heavy Weather*
April 1924	*Uncle Fred in the Springtime*
Late June 1924	*Full Moon*
August 1924	*Pigs Have Wings*
July 1925	*Service with a Smile*
Late August 1925	*Galahad at Blandings*
September 1925	'Birth of a Salesman'
July 1926	*A Pelican at Blandings*
July 1926	*Sunset at Blandings*

And we must not forget 'Sticky Wicket at Blandings', which could have occurred any time between August 1921 and July 1925.

13. The Legitimacy of Ronnie Fish

I. The Problem

Heavy Weather took place a few days after Lord Emsworth celebrated his sixtieth birthday, and *Leave it to Psmith* two years before that. There is one unconfirmed statement by Wodehouse that Lord Emsworth was born in 1859. But this statement must be rejected, because there is evidence from three different sources that *Leave it to Psmith* took place later than 1919, probably in 1921.[1] It follows that 1923 is the most likely date for *Heavy Weather*.

At the time of *Summer Lightning* and *Heavy Weather*, Ronnie Fish was aged twenty-five,[2] which means that he was born in 1898. But in that year (which was the year in which Galahad was shipped off to South Africa), Ronnie's mother was a child,[3] and his father was a dashing young subaltern, who in the previous year rode a bicycle down Piccadilly in sky-blue underclothing. He was still a subaltern in 1902, when, returning to his rooms in the early morning of New Year's Day, he mistook the coal-scuttle for a mad dog and tried to shoot it with the fire tongs. They did not marry until he was a stodgily respectable colonel,[4] which could hardly have been before 1910. So, if Ronnie was born in 1911, *Heavy Weather* must have taken place in 1936 – an impossibly late date.

II. The Critic Howarth's Solution

The critic Howarth solves the problem by suggesting that Ronnie's mother Lady Julia must have kicked over the traces: as a schoolgirl she must have succumbed to young Fishy Fish, and when later they legitimated Ronnie by getting married, she knew nothing of the sky-blue underclothing of 1897 or the coal-scuttle of 1902. 'The family evidently hushed it up', he says, 'and though Wodehouse must have suspected something I feel we should respect his discretion.'

III. Appraisal of Howarth's Theory

I fear that the critic Howarth overlooks the fact that legitimation by subsequent marriage was not introduced into English domestic law until January 1st 1927. (By 'English domestic law' I mean English law, minus its rules of the conflict of laws.) It is true that the Legitimacy Act 1926 provides that a child born before that date would be legitimated by a marriage celebrated before that date – but only from the commencement of the Act, i.e. January 1st 1927, which is an impossibly late date for *Heavy Weather*. However, legitimation by subsequent marriage was part of the law of Scotland long before 1927; and what is more, English rules of the conflict of laws recognised that a child legitimated under foreign law (including Scots law) was legitimated in England for most (but not all) purposes, provided that his father was domiciled in the foreign country both at the date of the child's birth and at the date of the subsequent marriage. So, if Fishy Fish was domiciled in Scotland at both these dates, Ronnie would have been recognised in England as having been legitimated (but he could not have succeeded to a peerage). But was he? I very much doubt it. There is no evidence that Ronnie's father was ever domiciled in Scotland; and Miles Fish does not sound to me like a Scottish name.

However, the critic Howarth's main point is not that Ronnie was legitimated by subsequent marriage, but that he was born illegitimate, at a time when his mother was a schoolgirl. What sort of girl was she? We can perhaps form some impression from a fascinating glimpse into the Blandings Castle nursery which Galahad vouchsafes to us:[5]

You always were a tough nut, Julia. Even as a child. It used to interest me in those days to watch you gradually dawning on the latest governess. I could have read her thoughts in her face, poor devil. First, she would meet Connie and you could almost hear her saying to herself 'Hello! A vicious specimen, this one'. And then you would come along, all wide, innocent blue eyes and flaxen curls, and she would feel a great wave of relief and fling her arms round you, thinking 'Well, here's one that's all right, thank God'. Little knowing that she had just come up against the stoniest-hearted, beastliest-natured, and generally most poisonous young human rattlesnake in all Shropshire.

Later Galahad tells Beach 'I saw her bite her governess once – in two places. And with just that serene angelic look on her face which she wore just now'.[6]

I do not know enough about child psychology even to guess from this evidence whether Lady Julia is likely to have had a youthful flirtation leading to the birth of an illegitimate child. The reader must form his own opinion. There are, however, two conversations in *Heavy Weather* which lead me to reject the theory that Ronnie was illegitimate. The first took place between Ronnie and his mother, soon after Ronnie's return from his cousin George's wedding in Norfolk. It was in the combination drawing-room and picture-gallery in which Blandings Castle was wont to assemble before the evening meal.[7] In reading this passage, and on the assumption that Ronnie was illegitimate, we need to bear in mind one probability and one certainty. The probability is that Ronnie at the age of twenty-five must have discovered that he was illegitimate. The certainty is that his mother must have realised that he might have discovered it. That being so, is it conceivable that she could have taken such a haughty line in that conversation? It is too long to quote verbatim, but two passages are particularly significant:

(i) There was a pause. Ronnie, who had just straightened his tie again, pulled it crooked and began straightening it once more. Lady Julia watched these manifestations of unrest with a grim blue stare. Ronnie, looking up and meeting it, diverted his gaze towards a portrait of the second Earl which hung on the wall beside him.

'Amazing beards those blokes used to wear,' he said nonchalantly.

'I wonder you can look your ancestors in the face.'

'I can't, as a matter of fact. They're an ugly crowd. The only decent one is Daredevil Dick Threepwood who married the actress.'

'You would bring up Daredevil Dick, wouldn't you?'

(ii) 'I take it that your idea when you marry is to settle down and lead a normal sort of life, and how are you going to have that with a chorus girl? How are you going to trust a woman of that sort of upbringing, who has lived on excitement ever since she was old enough to kick her beastly legs up in front of an audience and sees nothing wrong in going off and having affairs with every man that takes her fancy?'

How could Ronnie's mother possibly have said these things if (for all she knew) Ronnie might well have replied, 'Well, mother, unlike me Sue was born in wedlock, so the question is not whether she is good enough for me, but whether I am good enough for her?'

The second conversation was one between Galahad and Lady Julia:[8]

'When Miles Fish married you', said the Hon. Galahad, 'he was a respectable – even a stodgily respectable – Colonel. I remember your saying *the first time you met him*' [emphasis added] 'that you thought him slow. Believe me, Julia, when I knew dear old Fishy Fish as a young subaltern, while you were still poisoning governesses' lives at Blandings Castle, he was quite the reverse of slow. His jolly rapidity was the talk of London.'

And he proceeded to tell her about the sky-blue underclothing of 1897 and the coal-scuttle of 1902, and to inform her that 'supplementary material would be found in chapters 3, 11, 16, 17 and 21 – especially chapter 21'. But he did not threaten to include in his Reminiscences anything about Julia's youthful flirtation with Fishy Fish.

IV. CONCLUSION

I conclude that Ronnie Fish was legitimate and that the problem of the date of his birth is an insoluble one. It was, no doubt, one of those blunders which, as Wodehouse himself says, historians sometimes make.[9]

14. LORD EMSWORTH AND HIS FAMILY AND ENTOURAGE

I. THE LIFE OF LORD EMSWORTH

Lord Emsworth was born in 1863,[1] the eldest son of the eighth
Earl of Emsworth, who was killed in the hunting field at the age
of seventy-seven.[2] He was educated at Eton[3] but not, apparently,
at the University. He joined the Senior Conservative Club as a
country member in 1888.[4] At about the age of thirty he wore
long whiskers and held a commission in the Shropshire Yeo-
manry.[5] During the years when he held his commission his
country did not call to him to save her; but, had that call been
made, he would have answered it with as prompt a 'Bless my
soul! Of course. Certainly!' as any of his Crusader ancestors.[6]
(There was of course a call between 1898 and 1902; but Wodehouse did not believe in wars.) His wife died some time between
1900[7] and 1904[8] (the evidence is conflicting). It is not clear when
he came into the title. It must have been after 1898, because that
was the year when his father shipped Galahad off to South
Africa.[9] It was probably in 1899, when Galahad returned to
London. It is true that Vicky Underwood, the heroine of *Sunset
at Blandings*, says she met the eighth earl when she was a very
small child.[10] But, even if Wodehouse had left this statement
unrevised, it need cause no difficulty, because Vicky could have
been two years old in 1899 and yet only twenty-nine in *Sunset
at Blandings*. Lord Emsworth became a Justice of the Peace for
the county of Shropshire.[11] He visited Canada in 1898 or 1899[12]
and New York (twice) in 1925.[13]

He was bald, tall, thin, scraggy and had a slight stoop. He
grew a beard in 1922, but shaved it off when he discovered that
his younger son Freddie, in a false beard, looked like his father.[14]
He hated going to London or dressing up in smart clothes and

was usually to be seen in an old shooting coat with holes in the elbows. He was hardly ever rude to anyone, not even to his sister Constance. He was not at his best when conversing with younger members of the opposite sex, but he was very kind to Sue Brown, to the little cockney girl in 'Lord Emsworth and the Girl Friend', and to the doorstep sales girl in 'Birth of a Salesman'.

The only notable things he ever did in his life were to win prizes for roses, tulips,[15] pumpkins[16] and fat pigs (three times) at the Shropshire Agricultural Show.

II. LORD EMSWORTH'S FAMILY

Lord Emsworth had two sons, Viscount Bosham and the Hon. Freddie Threepwood, and one daughter, Lady Mildred Threepwood, who married Colonel Horace Mant. His elder son Viscount Bosham had two sons, James and George. Lord Emsworth was allergic to his younger son Freddie, whose presence at Blandings Castle jarred on him increasingly. And certainly Freddie's behaviour before his marriage was bound to cause pain to any father. He was expelled from Eton for breaking out at night and roaming the streets of Windsor in a false moustache. He was sent down from Oxford for pouring ink from a second-storey window on the Junior Dean of his College. He spent two years at an expensive London crammer and failed to pass into the Army. He twice ran up racing debts in London which his father had to pay, and was twice haled back to Blandings and had his allowance cut off.[17] He is introduced to us as 'a heavy, loutish-looking youth',[18] and we are not surprised when Aline Peters, his rich American fiancée, breaks the engagement and elopes with George Emerson.[19] He had no scruples about stealing valuable objects from his father[20] and his Aunt Constance.[21] He became a partner in a bookie's business.[22] The turning point in his life came when he married Niagara ('Aggie') Donaldson, only daughter of the proprietor of Donaldson's Dog Biscuits Inc. of Long Island, N.Y., and started working for that flourishing concern. For Aggie, or America, or both, made a man of Freddie, and converted him from a vapid, aimless youth with criminal tendencies into a reasonable human being, who was much liked by his female cousins and by his Uncle Galahad, and was quite a good dog-biscuit salesman.

Lord Emsworth had two brothers, Lancelot (who died before the Saga begins) and Galahad. Lancelot had a daughter, Millicent, who married Lord Emsworth's secretary, Hugo Carmody. Lord Emsworth had ten sisters: Lady Ann Warblington, Lady Constance Keeble, Lady Charlotte, Lady Hermione Wedge, Lady Georgiana Alcester, Lady Dora Garland, Lady Julia Fish, Lady Jane (who died before the Saga begins), Lady Florence Moresby and Lady Diana Phipps.

Lady Constance was twice married, once to Joseph Keeble, and once to Jimmy Schoonmaker, who were both elderly widowers. Joseph Keeble had a step-daughter Phyllis, who married Psmith's best friend, Mike Jackson. Jimmy Schoonmaker had a daughter Myra.

Lady Charlotte had a daughter Jane, who married George Abercrombie, a land agent.

Lady Hermione married Colonel Egbert Wedge. They had a daughter Veronica, who married Tipton Plimsoll, an American multi-millionaire.

Lady Georgiana Alcester had a son Percival, Lord Stockheath, and a daughter Gertrude, who married the Reverend Rupert Bingham.

Lady Dora married Sir Everard Garland, who died before the Saga begins. They had a daughter Prudence, who married Bill Lister, Galahad's godson.

Lady Julia married Major-General Sir Miles Fish, who died before the Saga begins. They had a son Ronald Overbury Fish, who married a chorus girl called Sue Brown, the daughter of Captain Jack Cotterleigh and of Galahad's old flame, Dolly Henderson.

Lady Jane had a daughter Angela, who married James Belford, and a son Wilfred Allsop, who married Monica Simmons, Lord Emsworth's pig-girl.

Lady Florence was twice married, once to J.B. Underwood, an American millionaire (who had a daughter called Vicky) and once to Kevin Moresby.

Lady Diana married Rollo Phipps, a big game hunter who was killed by a lion many years ago.

THREEPWOOD FAMILY TREE

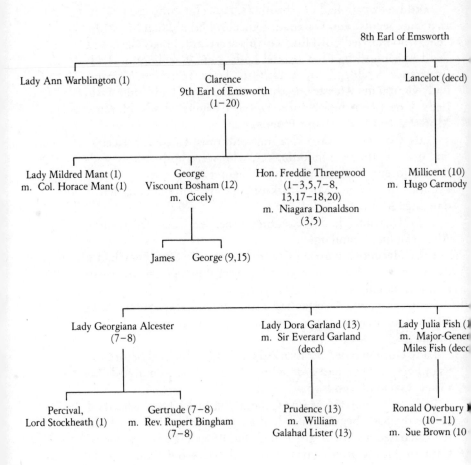

8th Earl of Emsworth

Lady Ann Warblington (1)

Clarence
9th Earl of Emsworth
(1–20)

Lancelot (decd)

Lady Mildred Mant (1)
m. Col. Horace Mant (1)

George
Viscount Bosham (12)
m. Cicely

Hon. Freddie Threepwood
(1–3,5,7–8,
13,17–18,20)
m. Niagara Donaldson
(3,5)

Millicent (10)
m. Hugo Carmody

James   George (9,15)

Lady Georgiana Alcester
(7–8)

Lady Dora Garland (13)
m. Sir Everard Garland
(decd)

Lady Julia Fish (
m. Major-Gener
Miles Fish (decc

Percival,
Lord Stockheath (1)

Gertrude (7–8)
m. Rev. Rupert Bingham
(7–8)

Prudence (13)
m. William
Galahad Lister (13)

Ronald Overbury
(10–11)
m. Sue Brown (10

1 – *Something Fresh*
2 – *Leave it to Psmith*
3 – 'The Custody of the Pumpkin'
4 – 'Lord Emsworth and the Girl Friend'
5 – 'Lord Emsworth Acts for the Best'

6 – 'Pig-hoo-o-o-o-ey!'
7 – 'Company for Gertrude'
8 – 'The Go-Getter'
9 – 'The Crime Wave at Blandings'
10 – *Summer Lightning*

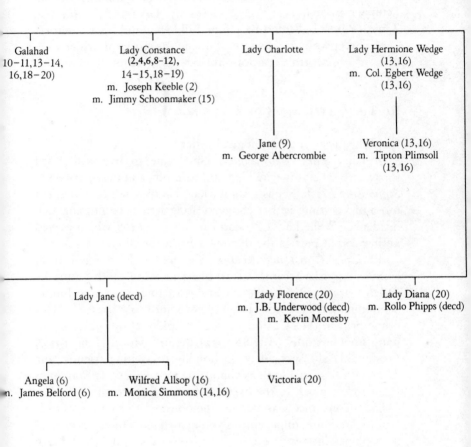

Galahad
10-11,13-14,
16,18-20)

Lady Constance
(2,4,6,8-12),
14-15,18-19)
m. Joseph Keeble (2)
m. Jimmy Schoonmaker (15)

Lady Charlotte

Lady Hermione Wedge
(13,16)
m. Col. Egbert Wedge
(13,16)

Jane (9)
m. George Abercrombie

Veronica (13,16)
m. Tipton Plimsoll
(13,16)

Lady Jane (decd)

Lady Florence (20)
m. J.B. Underwood (decd)
m. Kevin Moresby

Lady Diana (20)
m. Rollo Phipps (decd)

Angela (6)
m. James Belford (6)

Wilfred Allsop (16)
m. Monica Simmons (14,16)

Victoria (20)

Lord Emsworth thus had two grandsons (James and George), three nephews (Lord Stockheath, Ronnie and Wilfred), six nieces (Millicent, Jane, Veronica, Gertrude, Prudence and Angela), two nieces by marriage (Sue Brown and Monica Simmons) and six nephews by marriage (Hugo Carmody, George Abercrombie, Tipton Plimsoll, Rupert Bingham, Bill Lister and James Belford.

A Threepwood family tree, showing the stories in which each of Lord Emsworth's relations appears, is given on the previous page.

III. The Chatelaines of Blandings

Here they are, in chronological order:

(i) *Lady Anne Warblington.* She came to live with Lord Emsworth when his wife died and held office in one story only, *Something Fresh.* She is a somewhat shadowy figure. She spent most of her time in her room, writing letters or nursing sick headaches.[23] She had a Persian cat called Muriel which played an important part in the denouement of the plot.[24]

(ii) *Lady Constance Keeble.* She had a long reign from eighteen months before the start of *Leave it to Psmith*[25] until the end of *Service with a Smile*, when she became engaged to Jimmy Schoonmaker,[26] i.e. from January 1919 until July 1925. She does not appear in 'The Custody of the Pumpkin' (July 1921), 'Company for Gertrude' (August 1922) or *Full Moon* (June 1924). Presumably she was away on holiday or visiting friends. She returned for a brief spell as chatelaine in *A Pelican at Blandings* (July 1926), much to the disgust of Lord Emsworth.

Lady Constance was a snob. She objected to parsons' sons,[27] land agents[28] and impecunious young men like Hugo Carmody[29] as nephews-in-law or even as step-step-sons-in-law;[30] she also objected to chorus girls as nieces-in-law.[31] She bullied Lord Emsworth unmercifully. As he bitterly reflected, 'one might bluster and one might struggle, one might raise hands to heaven and clench fists and shake them, but in the end the result was always the same – Connie got what she wanted'.[32] Sue Brown quailed before her.[33] So did Valerie Twistleton (a much stronger character).[34] Ronnie Fish said she had to be seen to be believed. Hugo Carmody paled beneath his tan as he spoke of her. Monty

Bodkin strongly suspected that she conducted human sacrifices at the time of the full moon.[35] Yet she could sometimes behave with discretion. At the end of *Uncle Fred in the Springtime*, Lord Ickenham talked himself out of a sticky situation by asserting (quite falsely) that Lord Emsworth was infatuated with a girl of humble origin young enough to be his grand-daughter.[36] But Lady Constance must have either resisted the temptation to upbraid her brother for his folly, or she must have concealed the identity of her informant. Otherwise, Lord Emsworth would never have invited Lord Ickenham to the Castle again only fifteen months later.[37] And, as we shall see, Lady Constance did not hesitate to engage a female secretary and a female pig-minder for her brother.

Lord Ickenham was convinced that Lord Emsworth would be a happier man, and Blandings a happier place, if she left the Castle: so he did what he could to foster her romance with Jimmy Schoonmaker.[38] She married him in New York, and Lord Emsworth attended the wedding.[39] There are two mysteries here: first, why was the chatelaine of Blandings not married in state from the Castle? And secondly, how did she manage to persuade poor Clarence to travel to New York for the wedding, only a week or two before the Agricultural Show?

(iii) *Lady Hermione Wedge*. Unlike the rest of the female members of her family, who were tall and stately, Lady Hermione Wedge was short and dumpy and looked like a cook – in her softer moods, a cook well satisfied with her latest soufflé; when stirred to anger, a cook about to give notice; but always a cook of strong character.[40] Nobody who knew her would have doubted that Constance was an able disciplinarian, but they would have been obliged to concede that she could not be considered in Hermione's class. Hermoine began where she left off.[41]

Lady Hermione was in charge at Blandings in *Full Moon*, during one of Lady Constance's temporary absences. Just over a year later, she took advantage of Lord Emsworth's absence in New York attending Constance's wedding to move in permanently.[42] But Galahad adroitly got rid of her.[43]

(iv) *Lady Florence Moresby*. She was an angular woman with a bearing so erect that she gave the impression of having swallowed a poker.[44] She was in charge in *Sunset at Blandings*.

IV. LORD EMSWORTH'S SECRETARIES

Here they are, in chronological order:

(i) *Rupert Baxter*. He held office throughout *Something Fresh* and through most of *Leave it to Psmith*, but was sacked for throwing flower pots into Lord Emsworth's bedroom in the small hours of the morning.[45] From that time on, Lord Emsworth was convinced that Baxter was insane (a conclusion to which Lord Emsworth's son-in-law, Colonel Horace Mant, had already come seven years before[46]). But Lady Constance, Baxter's staunch ally and only friend at the Castle, was always plotting to get him back. She once succeeded in having him engaged as tutor to Lord Emsworth's grandson George in the middle of the summer holidays,[47] and once in having him back at the Castle as a guest.[48]

Baxter had a somewhat chequered career as a secretary. Before entering Lord Emsworth's employment, he was secretary to Sir Ralph Dillingworth, a Yorkshire baronet – an odd sort of fellow who shot mice in the drawing-room with an elephant gun, and became a patient of Sir Roderick Glossop.[49] In between *Something Fresh* and *Leave it to Psmith*, Baxter was employed by Mr Horace Jevons, an American millionaire – for how long, we do not know, but the period included December 1918 and January 1919.[50] He then re-entered Lord Emsworth's employment, but, as stated above, was sacked at the end of *Leave it to Psmith*, and was employed again by Jevons. However, in 'The Crime Wave at Blandings', he had just left Jevons, who had to return to America, while Baxter did not want to leave England.[51] This piece of news greatly upset Lord Emsworth, who had never met that genial Chicagoan, but had always thought kindly and gratefully of him, as one does of some great doctor who has succeeded in isolating and confining a disease germ. At the end of 'The Crime Wave at Blandings', Baxter leaves the Castle, burning with resentment because he had been peppered with shots from an airgun by Lord Emsworth's grandson George, by Lord Emsworth himself, and by Beach. But he returned as a guest at the beginning of *Summer Lightning*, at Lady Constance's urgent invitation.[52] At the end of that story he left to rejoin his former employer, Horace Jevons, sincerely hoping that he would never set eyes on any of the Threepwoods again.[53] But he returned to Blandings as secretary to the Duke of Dunstable in *Uncle Fred in the Springtime*. We last hear of him in *Galahad at Blandings*, when he was employed by an American millionaire (presumably Jevons, though the fact is not stated) in Pittsburgh, Pennsylvania.[54]

(ii) *Ronald Eustace Rupert Psmith*. He succeeded Baxter at the end of *Leave it to Psmith*,[55] but is mentioned no more, not even when the tale of Lord Emsworth's secretaries is told in later stories in order to set the record straight.

(iii) *Hugo Carmody*. He was secretary for eleven weeks,[56] which included the period of *Summer Lightning*. He left at the end of that story to marry Lord Emsworth's niece Millicent.[57]

(iv) *Monty Bodkin*. He was engaged by Lady Constance at the beginning of *Heavy Weather*,[58] but was sacked because Lord Emsworth suspected that Monty was a tool of his uncle, Sir Gregory Parsloe-Parsloe, and had designs on the Empress of Blandings.[59]

(v) *Gerald Anstruther Vail*. He was the nephew of Galahad's old friend Plug Basham, and held office during *Pigs Have Wings*.[60] He married Penelope Donaldson, the younger daughter of Freddie's father-in-law, who had only one daughter ('Aggie') when she married Freddie three years before.[61]

(vi) *Lavender Briggs*. She was a graduate of the London School of Economics[62] and held office during the early part of *Service with a Smile*, having been engaged by Lady Constance.[63] Lord Emsworth thought she was the worst secretary he ever had, worse even than Baxter.[64] She was sacked for plotting to steal the Empress of Blandings.[65]

(vii) *Sandy Callender*. She held office during *Galahad at Blandings*, but left to marry Galahad's protegé, Sam Bagshott.[66] Lord Emsworth thought she was an insufferable pest, worse than Baxter or Lavinia Briggs, because she was so efficient.[67]

The only one of his secretaries whom Lord Emsworth really liked was Hugo Carmody, because he was sound on pigs[68] and left him alone and didn't fuss him.[69] Lord Emsworth's ideal secretary would have been one who breakfasted in bed, dozed in an armchair through the morning, played golf in the afternoon and took the rest of the day off.[70]

V. LORD EMSWORTH'S PIG-MINDERS

Here they are:

(i) *George Cyril Wellbeloved*. He was the first, the youngest and the most articulate of Lord Emsworth's pigmen. He was only twenty-nine when we first meet him in 'Pig-hoo-o-o-o-ey!', when he was arrested for being drunk and disorderly in the tap-room of the Goat and Feathers at Market Blandings, and very properly jugged for fourteen days without the option of a fine. Three years later his niece Marlene Wellbeloved, was employed as a barmaid at the Emsworth Arms.[71]

George Cyril Wellbeloved was a tall, red-haired man with a squint[72] and a broken nose, the former bestowed on him at birth, the latter acquired in the course of a political discussion at the Goose and Gander in Market Blandings in which he had es-poused the communist cause.[73] He was certainly articulate, and no respecter of persons. He addressed Beach[74] and Lord Em-sworth[75] as 'cocky', and only just managed to stop himself (when in an advanced stage of intoxication) from doing the same to his employer, Sir Gregory Parsloe-Parsloe.[76]

He was lured away from Lord Emsworth's service in return for a promise of higher wages by Lord Emsworth's neighbour and rival pig-breeder, Sir Gregory Parsloe-Parsloe. There is a conflict of testimony as to when this act of treachery took place. One account says it was shortly after the Empress won her first silver medal,[77] which she did in late July 1922. Another says it was 'earlier in the summer' in which *Summer Lightning* takes place,[78] which was late July 1923.

He returned to Lord Emsworth's service not long before the beginning of *Service with a Smile*,[79] replacing Monica Simmons, but was dismissed for his part in Lavender Briggs' plot to steal the Empress.[80] Later in the same story he was taken back again, because Lord Emsworth considered that no pigman he had ever had understood the Empress as Wellbeloved did.[81] But he was dismissed a second time with contumely.[82] We are not told the reason for this second dismissal, merely that it had taken place; but the reason must have been a grave one, because flame flashed from Lord Emsworth's pince-nez. Wellbeloved retired from his profession at the early age of thirty-two, having inherited from a relative a prosperous public house in Wolverhampton.

(ii) *James (or Percy) Pirbright*. He succeeded George Cyril Wellbeloved when Sir Gregory Parsloe-Parsloe lured him away, and fortunately the Empress took to him from the first.[83] He held office in *Summer Lightning* and *Heavy Weather* and may have been the anonymous pigman in *Uncle Fred in the Springtime*.[84] He was tall and thin and scraggy, even more so than his employer.[85] In *Heavy Weather* he distinguished himself by incarcerating Lord Tilbury in a potting-shed because he thought he was trying to poison the Empress with a potato, and later found Lord Tilbury near the sty, overpowered him, rolled him in the mud and incarcerated him in the coal-cellar.[86] Pirbright, unlike Wellbeloved, was not an articulate man. When he said 'Gur!' he meant 'You come along with me and I'll shut you up somewhere while I go and inform his lordship of what has occurred'.[87] He was last heard of in Canada.[88]

(iii) *Edwin Pott*. He held office in *Full Moon*. He was a little gnome of a man with no roof to his mouth who smelled worse than the Empress.[89] He was well stricken in years and might have been either a smelly centenarian or an octogenarian who had been prematurely aged by trouble. His vocal chords had never been the same since the evening during the last General Election when he had strained them while addressing the crowd at the public bar of the Emsworth Arms in the Conservative interest.[90] He retired into private life after winning a football pool.[91]

(iv) *Monica Simmons*. She was a large, muscular girl, one of the six daughters of a rural vicar, all of whom had played hockey for Roedean. She was engaged by Lady Constance[92] and held office during *Pigs Have Wings* and *Galahad at Blandings*. We are not told whether she was related to old Simmons, who was once Lord Emsworth's land agent;[93] probably not, because she was a cousin of Sir Gregory Parsloe-Parsloe.[94] This relationship naturally made Lord Emsworth suspicious of her at first; and he thought that her habit of referring to the Empress as a 'piggy-wiggy' betrayed a lack of reverence. As Galahad said, it was the wrong tone and seemed to show that the child was too frivolous in her outlook to hold so responsible a post. The girl, he pointed out, who carelessly dismisses a three-times silver medallist at the Shropshire Agricultural Show as a 'piggy-wiggy' today is a girl who may quite easily forget to give the noble animal lunch tomorrow.[95] But Lord Emsworth came to realise that Monica Simmons was a worthy daughter of the agricultural college from which she had graduated, and learnt to trust her implicitly.[96] She left to marry Lord Emsworth's nephew Wilfred Allsop.[97]

(v) *Cuthbert Price*. He held office during *A Pelican at Blandings*,[98] but all we know about him is his name.

VI. The Empress of Blandings

No essay on Lord Emsworth and his entourage would be complete without a short section on his prize-winning pig. He was never happier than when, draped bonelessly over the rail of her sty like a wet sock, he watched her taking nourishment. Even when she had retired for the night and was no longer visible, he used to spend hours at her sty listening to her breathing.[99]

The Empress had a somewhat chequered career, for in the intervals between winning her three silver medals in the Fat Pigs class at the Shropshire Agricultural Show, she was constantly being stolen – sometimes by impecunious nephews, anxious to ingratiate themselves with Lord Emsworth when they 'found' her again; sometimes by minions of Sir Gregory Parsloe-Parsloe, Lord Emsworth's neighbour and rival pig-breeder, or of the Duke of Dunstable, his uninvited guest. In *Summer Lightning*, Ronnie Fish stole the Empress and hid her in the game-keeper's cottage in the west wood, where she was found by Hugo Carmody and Millicent and removed to Baxter's caravan.[100] In *Heavy Weather*, Ronnie Fish, assisted by Beach, again stole the Empress and put her in the dickey of Ronnie's two-seater, in order to blackmail Lord Emsworth into giving him his money. (It was only then that Galahad, himself a pig-stealer in the days of his youth, began to understand what Sue Brown saw in Ronnie Fish.[101]) In *Uncle Fred in the Springtime*, Baxter stole the Empress and put her in the Duke of Dunstable's bedroom.[102] In *Full Moon*, Galahad removed the Empress from her sty and put her in Veronica Wedge's bedroom in order to induce Tipton Plimsoll to propose to her.[103] In *Pigs Have Wings*, George Cyril Wellbeloved (employed by Sir Gregory Parsloe-Parsloe) stole the Empress and put her in Queen of Matchingham's sty, whence she was removed by Galahad and put in the kitchen of a house on the Shrewsbury road.[104]

We have seen how the Empress with her three silver medals is a key figure in the chronology of the Porcine Period. How was it that in *Galahad at Blandings*, which took place in the second half of August, when the Shropshire Show must have been imminent, she was not only not expected to win her fourth medal, but apparently was not even entered as a competitor? The explanation, though surprising, is quite simple. Shortly before that story began, Lord Emsworth's favourite author changed his name by deed poll from Whiffle to Whipple,[105] and brought out a new edition of his magnum opus on *The Care of the Pig*, in which he recommended a reduction of no less than 90 per cent in the daily diet of pigs. In earlier editions, that noble chapter about swill and bran-mash with its perfect prose[106] recommended a diet of 57,800 calories a day.[107] But the new edition recommended one of only 5,700 calories.[108] Such a violent reduction in diet could not have been tolerated by any pig of spirit, let alone a silver medallist with two bars. The poor animal must have lost weight and pined until she was no match for the Queen, or even the outclassed Pride, of Matchingham. It is possible that, if Lord Emsworth had been at Blandings at the critical time, he might have had the resolution to reject Whipple's fanciful new doctrine on diet. But alas! he was in New York in mid-August, attending Constance's wedding. Presumably, he left Monica Simmons in charge; unlike Wellbeloved, Pirbright or Pott, she was college-trained, and therefore more inclined to rely on books than on common sense. And when Lord Emsworth returned, the damage was already done. It must have been a poignant moment. We are grateful to Wodehouse for tactfully drawing a veil over this sad ending of a fine career.

15. GALAHAD THREEPWOOD, MAN ABOUT TOWN

It was a stroke of genius on the part of Wodehouse to give Lord Emsworth a brother like Galahad. With his quick wit and ready tongue he was a perfect foil to the rambling, doddering ninth earl. With his catholic taste in friends he was also a perfect foil to his snob sisters Constance, Julia, Dora and Hermione, all of whom considered him a blot on the family escutcheon.[1] But other more discerning observers thought that he was the only genuinely distinguished member of the family.[2] As he himself modestly put it in 1924, England had been ringing with his name for thirty years.[3]

He was born in 1867 and so was four years younger than Lord Emsworth.[4] After coming down from Oxford he joined the Pelican club and spent his twenties and thirties painting London red with his aristocratic cronies. He must have been introduced to Albert Edward, Prince of Wales, for how else can we explain his invitation to a Buckingham Palace Garden Party in 1906?[5] He was constantly being arrested for being drunk and disorderly and often spent the night in Vine Street police station.[6] It was his boast in later years that it always took at least two policemen to arrest him and one more to carry his hat.[7] Although he was a frequent visitor to New York,[8] he was (oddly enough, as he put it) never arrested there, though he was once arrested in Paris and did not enjoy the experience.[9]

He is introduced to us in 1923 as a short, trim, dapper little man of the type one associates with check suits, tight trousers, grey bowler hats, pink carnations and race-glasses bumping against the left hip.[10] He always wore a black-rimmed monocle.[11] One of the first things people noticed about him was his extraordinarily good health. Wan contemporaries who had once painted London red in his company were now doomed to an existence of dry toast, Vichy water and German cure resorts;[12] but Galahad had discovered the prime secret of eternal youth – to keep the decanter circulating and never to go to bed before four in the morning.[13]

When, in 1923, it became known that he was writing his Reminiscences, panic seized the more elderly of the nobility and gentry all over England, not least Sir Gregory Parsloe-Parsloe, Lord Emsworth's nearest neighbour.[14] The publication of this book might well have rocked civilisation, if only the manuscript had not been eaten by the Empress of Blandings. But fortunately Gally was a racy and compulsive raconteur[15] and he tells us a good many stories which would have appeared in his book, sometimes many times over. Some of these stories have been mentioned in an earlier chapter because they are precisely dated and so help to establish the chronology of the Blandings Castle Saga. One of the most intriguing ones which has not yet been mentioned (because it is not dated) is the story of Sir Gregory Parsloe-Parsloe and the prawns. Gally first threatened to include this story in his book when he suspected that 'young Parsloe' had stolen the Empress; and Parsloe uttered a sharp cry and turned a deep magenta.[16] Gally entrusted his manuscript to Beach the butler for safe custody; Beach began to read it and was soon chuckling softly, like a vast kettle coming to the boil. When he got to the story of the prawns he fairly let himself go: 'HA .... HOR .... HOO!' he roared.[17] No wonder that when Parsloe, deep in conference at Blandings with Constance and Julia, moved heavily to the window and stood looking out into the night, it seemed to him that across the starry sky he could see written in letters of fire the story of the prawns.[18] Alas! we are never told this famous story. The nearest we get to it is at the end of *Summer Lightning*, when Gally begins to tell the story to Sue Brown: 'It was at Ascot, the year Martingale won the Gold Cup. Young Parsloe....' And then the curtain falls.

Some of Gally's former drinking cronies appear in the Saga. The one who plays the biggest role is Parsloe, whom Gally never really liked and with whom he ceased to be on cordial terms after the winter of 1906.[19] Then there was Major (Plug) Basham, the uncle of Gerald Vail, one of Lord Emsworth's secretaries.[20] Plug Basham figures in many of Gally's best stories, notably the one in which the stolen pig was put in Plug's bedroom, and the one in which Plug threw a side of beef at Romano's and stunned Stinker Pyke (later Lord Tilbury, the would-be publisher of Gally's Reminiscences) into unconsciousness.[21] Plug was dead at the time of *Heavy Weather*[22] but seems to have come to life again a year later in *Pigs Have Wings*.[23] Gally had not met Stinker Pyke for twenty-five years, and Lord Tilbury naturally objected to being addressed by a nickname which even in his youth was offensive to him. Gally expressed concern when told that Pyke's name was Tilbury: 'Going about under a false name? Bad. I don't like that. It never pays.'[24] Another crony is that mysterious figure Fruity Biffen, who in *Full Moon* hadn't stirred abroad without a false beard for years, because his relations with the bookies were always a bit strained,[25] but who, in *Pigs Have Wings*, turns out to be an Admiral.[26] ('Fruity' is of course a typical naval nickname.) The Admiral took a furnished villa called Sunnybrae just outside Market Blandings on the Shrewsbury Road.[27] He liked telling long stories about life on the China station in the old days. In the Emsworth Arms he found a ready listener in George Cyril Wellbeloved, Parsloe's pig man, for whom no story could be too long to listen to provided free beer was supplied, as on these occasions it always was. Admiral Biffen even invited Wellbeloved to Sunnybrae and gave him bottles of beer.[28]

Gally was an amiable man. Everybody loved him except his sisters and 'young Parsloe'. He was extremely fond of his brother Clarence;[29] and Clarence found Gally a great comfort to him, especially when he was being bullied by one of his sisters.[30] Yet Gally could be stern and even rude at times. He was gloriously rude to people he disliked, such as his sister Julia,[31] his sister Constance[32] and Parsloe.[33] He could even be rude to people he liked, such as his nephews Freddie Threepwood[34] and Ronnie Fish,[35] if he thought they had done something silly or unkind. On one occasion Ronnie Fish, at the age of ten, put tin-tacks on Gally's chair; Gally pursued him to the roof of Blandings Castle and chased him twenty-seven times round a chimney-stack with a whangee.[36] Fifteen years later, Ronnie tells Gally that Sue Brown must be in love with Monty Bodkin because she spent the afternoon with him on the roof. 'I was up on that roof with you once' retorted Gally 'but if you thought I was in love with you you must have been singularly obtuse'.[37]

Gally wasted his substance in riotous living in the days of his youth, so it is not surprising that in his fifties he was a poor man, subsisting on a younger son's allowance from the estate.[38] Yet poverty is a relative term, and Gally certainly was not destitute. When not visiting Blandings he lived in a fashionable part of London (Duke Street, St James's and Berkeley Mansions); he owned a car and employed a chauffeur to drive it,[39] though he could drive perfectly well himself.[40]

Like Bertie Wooster, Gally could not abide sundered hearts.[41] Anyone who was connected with him however remotely could rely on his help if it was needed to make the course of true love run more smoothly. There was Sue Brown, the daughter of his old flame Dolly Henderson, in *Summer Lightning* and *Heavy Weather*; his godsons Bill Lister, in *Full Moon*, and John Halliday in *A Pelican at Blandings*; Sam Bagshot, the son of his old friend Boko Bagshot, in *Galahad at Blandings*; Jerry Vail, the nephew of his old friend Plug Basham, in *Pigs Have Wings*; and Tipton Plimsoll, the nephew of another old friend, Chet Tipton, in *Full Moon* and *Galahad at Blandings*. One of Galahad's most impudent feats was to introduce Bill Lister into the Castle on no less than three separate occasions: once as an artist to paint the Empress, once as a gardener disguised in Fruity Biffen's beard, and once as another artist called Landseer, because Lord Emsworth admired his Stag at Bay.[42] He was sacked by Lord Emsworth, because his portrait of the pig made her look intoxicated; sacked as a gardener by Lady Hermione Wedge, because he mistook her for the cook and tipped her half a crown to deliver a note to her niece Prudence, with whom he was in love; and expelled as a guest by Hermione, because Freddie Threepwood carelessly revealed his true identity.[43]

But Gally's greatest triumph was to overcome the determined opposition of his sisters Constance and Julia to the engagement between Ronnie Fish and Sue Brown, the chorus girl. He had to do this twice, once in *Summer Lightning* and again in *Heavy Weather*. He did it in *Summer Lightning* by promising not to publish his Reminiscences if Constance would withdraw her opposition to the engagement. It was a terrible wrench to Gally to have to sacrifice his magnum opus in this way for the sake of Sue's happiness.[44] But he decided to do so after making sure that Sue really was in love with Ronnie.[45] Yet there is something unconvincing about the end of *Summer Lightning*. Not only does Gally's big scene with Constance take place off stage, but also it should surely have been obvious to him that Constance would not keep her side of the bargain and would plot with others to get the manuscript destroyed, which would mean that Gally's scope for blackmail would be at an end. And so there had to be a sequel, *Heavy Weather*.

Gally becomes more and more like Lord Ickenham as the Blandings Saga progresses. In the later stories there is no one like him for telling the tale. It seems a pity that he and Uncle Fred never appeared together in the same book, for it would have been interesting to see who would outwit the other. And yet perhaps it is just as well: the mixture might have been too rich.

16. THE THREEPWOOD SETTLED ESTATES

I. THE LIFE AND ENTAILED INTERESTS

To the outside world, it must have seemed as if Clarence, ninth earl of Emsworth, was the owner of Blandings Castle. The same impression must have been sustained by most of his guests – but not by the Duke of Dunstable, Lord Ickenham or Sir Gregory Parsloe-Parsloe, who like Lord Emsworth were landowners. Lord Emsworth's two grandsons, his three nephews, his six nieces, his six nephews-in-law and his two nieces-in-law[1] must all have thought the same. So must his secretaries, except perhaps the Efficient Baxter and Lavender Briggs, if they had studied law. So must his pig-minders and his numerous indoor and outdoor staff. (The little cockney girl in 'Lord Emsworth and the Girl Friend' thought that Angus McAllister was 'the old josser the plice belongs to', but she was a special case.)

All these people would have been wrong. Lord Emsworth was not the owner of Blandings Castle. As Sir Frederick Pollock said:

> The lord of this mansion is named by all men its owner; it is said to belong to him; the park, the demesne, the farms are called his. But we shall be almost safe in assuming that he is not the full and free owner of any part of it. He is a 'limited owner', having an interest only for his own life. He might have become the full owner if he had possessed the means of waiting, the independence of thought and will to break the tradition of his order and the bias of his education, and the energy to persevere in his dissent against the counsels and feelings of his family.[2] But he had every inducement to let things go their accustomed way. Those whom he had always trusted told him, and probably with sincere belief, that the accustomed way was the best for the family, for the land, for the tenants and for the country. And there could be no doubt that it was at the time the most agreeable to himself.[3]

Unless the Threepwood family managed its affairs differently from every other landed aristocratic family in England, Lord Emsworth was not the owner of Blandings. He was no more than tenant for life. What lawyers call the fee simple must have been in abeyance for centuries – perhaps since the original creation of the earldom. For Blandings Castle must have been the subject of a strict settlement; and under the strict settlement, at the time of the Saga, the limitations would have been as follows:

(i) to Clarence, the ninth Earl, for life;

(ii) remainder to his elder son, Viscount Bosham, for life;

(iii) remainder to Viscount Bosham's first and other sons successively according to seniority in tail male (he had two, James and George);

(iv) remainder to Lord Emsworth's younger son, Freddie Threepwood, for life;

(v) remainder to Freddie's first and other sons successively according to seniority in tail male (he had none);

(vi) remainder to Lord Emsworth's brother, Galahad Threepwood, for life;

(vii) remainder to Galahad's first and other sons successively according to seniority in tail male (he had none);

(viii) remainder to Viscount Bosham in fee simple.

There would have been no life interest limited to Lord Emsworth's daughter Mildred or to his ten sisters, and no entailed interests limited to their children, because the earldom was no doubt limited to the first earl and the heirs male of his body, and it was naturally desirable that the Castle should devolve in the same way as the title.

II. THE PORTIONS

Under the strict settlement, portions (capital sums secured by a long term of years vested in trustees) would have been payable to Lord Emsworth's sisters and his two younger brothers, Lancelot and Galahad, and to his daughter Mildred and his younger son Freddie, as and when each of them attained the age of twenty-one or being female married under that age. These portions were intended to start the younger sons in life and to provide marriage portions for the daughters. With such a wealthy family, the amount of the portions must have been considerable. How, then, are we to account for the perennial poverty of Galahad and Freddie?

In *Full Moon*, Galahad tells his godson Bill Lister (who needed capital) 'I wish I could supply some. I'd give it to you like a shot if I had it, but I subsist on a younger son's allowance from the estate'.[4] In *Pigs Have Wings*, when Penelope Donaldson tries to touch him for £2,000 so that she can marry her impecunious boy friend, he tells her 'My child, I'm a pauper. I'm a younger son. In English families, the heir scoops in the jackpot and all the runners-up get are the few crumbs that fall from his table.'[5] (There he was entirely wrong, for it was much more common for the heir to be crippled by having to pay mortgage interest for portions which had been injudiciously fixed at a larger amount than the estate could really stand.) The explanation must be that Galahad ran through the whole of his portion while he was sowing his wild oats in the 1890s, and so was dependent in later life on the generosity of his elder brother.

Freddie's case is much more difficult. The eighth earl had thirteen children, the ninth earl only three, so Freddie's portion must have been much larger than Galahad's was a generation before. Yet in *Something Fresh*, Freddie is reduced to stealing a scarab from his father in order to buy off a chorus girl who, he wrongly thinks, is threatening to sue him for breach of promise.[6] In *Leave it to Psmith*, he is reduced to stealing his Aunt Constance's necklace in order to buy a share in a bookie's business.[7] At the start of both stories, he has been haled back to Blandings and had his allowance cut off because he ran up racing debts in London which his father had to pay.[8] His financial affairs were on an extremely unstable footing before his marriage. He was a much younger man than Galahad was at the time of the two conversations recorded above. What became of his portion? It can hardly all have gone on racing debts, and he does not appear to have had any other expensive tastes. The only explanation I can offer is that Wodehouse did not understand the mechanism of a strict settlement (and who shall blame him?). He would not have recognised a strict settlement if you brought it to him on a plate with watercress round it.

III. LORD EMSWORTH'S TRUSTEESHIPS

Lord Emsworth was trustee for his niece Angela, the daughter of his deceased sister Jane; and for his nephew Ronnie Fish, the only son of his sister Julia and her deceased husband Major-General Sir Miles Fish. In addition, he seems to have had some mysterious power to prevent the marriage of his niece Millicent, the daughter of his deceased brother Lancelot. These three cases all have some odd features; let us look at each of them in turn.

(i) *Angela*. In 'Pig-hoo-o-o-o-ey!' Lady Constance Keeble reminds Lord Emsworth that 'when poor Jane died' she left him Angela's trustee; and Angela tells him that she can't touch her money without his consent until she's twenty-five, and she is now twenty-one. Evidently, Lady Jane made Lord Emsworth Angela's trustee in her last will; and evidently she was married without a marriage settlement, otherwise she would have had no money of her own to leave. But if she postponed vesting until Angela attained the age of twenty-five, what right had any trustee to part with the money before that date? The answer may perhaps be that the will contained a power of advancement empowering the trustee to advance not more than half his or her presumptive share to any beneficiary before he or she obtained a vested interest in the trust property. Section 32 of the Trustee Act 1925 would of course not have been applicable, because Jane died well before that Act came into operation on 1 January 1926.

(ii) *Ronnie Fish*. Ronnie Fish was twenty-five at the time of *Summer Lightning* and *Heavy Weather*,[9] and Lord Emsworth was his trustee. The plot of both stories hinges on whether Lord Emsworth will give him his money so that he can marry Sue Brown. The trust property must have been Fish money, not Threepwood money, and must have been derived from the will of Ronnie's father. This is partly for the simple reason that Ronnie's mother was alive, and partly for the more complex reason that the Rule against Perpetuities would have invalidated any gift contained in their marriage settlement to any of Julia's and Miles' children, if vesting was postponed to a greater age than twenty-one.

Lord Emsworth was induced to part with £500 to enable Ronnie to buy a half share in the Hot Spot night club. This happened about a year before *Summer Lightning*, when Ronnie would have been twenty-four. The Hot Spot folded up after seven weeks,[10] and the £500 went down the drain. At the end of *Heavy Weather*, Constance and Julia between them nearly succeed in persuading Lord Emsworth not to advance any more money to Ronnie, but Ronnie and Galahad outwit them. Now, if Ronnie was entitled to a vested interest in the trust property when he attained the age of twenty-five, what right had Lord Emsworth to refuse to disgorge it? I can only surmise that Ronnie's father had such a low opinion of his son's financial acumen that he postponed vesting until Ronnie attained some greater age. In that case we must assume that the will contained a power of advancement, and that it was in exercise of that power that Lord Emsworth at last signed the cheque.

(iii) *Millicent*. It is taken for granted in *Summer Lightning* that Millicent cannot marry Hugo Carmody unless Lord Emsworth gives his consent.[11] There is no suggestion that money was any obstacle, though it is true that Hugo had prospects of future wealth rather than any immediate source of income apart from his secretaryship: he was the heir to an entailed estate in Worcestershire.[12] The only obstacle was the supposed need for Lord Emsworth's consent. But he would have had no right to refuse his consent unless Lancelot had appointed him Millicent's guardian and Millicent was under twenty-one. But was she? I very much doubt it; she seems more mature than Sue Brown, who was twenty. If she was of full age, what was all the fuss about?

I. THE RIVER, THE WREKIN AND THE ROAD

Blandings Castle stands upon a knoll of rising ground at the southern end of the celebrated Vale of Blandings in the county of Shropshire. Away in the blue distance wooded hills run down to where the Severn gleams like an unsheathed sword; while up from the river rolling parkland, mounting and dipping, surges in a green wave almost to the castle walls.[1] Although these distant hills are often stressed in descriptions of the view,[2] from the rose garden the Wrekin is the only hill in sight.[3]

It is one of the largest houses in England,[4] and was built in the early Tudor period.[5] No, I'm wrong; it is one of the oldest inhabited houses in England,[6] and in the Middle Ages was an impregnable fortress.[7] Sorry, wrong again; it came into existence towards the middle of the fifteenth century.[8]

In the Preface to the 1969 edition of *Something Fresh* Wodehouse says: 'When I wrote *Something Fresh* I rashly placed Blandings Castle in Shropshire, because my happiest days as a boy were spent near Bridgnorth, overlooking the fact that to get to the heart of Shropshire by train takes four hours'. But oddly enough, there is no mention from beginning to end of *Something Fresh* that Blandings Castle is in Shropshire. On the contrary, Wodehouse seems to go out of his way to tell us that it is *not* in Shropshire, for he refers to 'distant Much Middlefold, Salop' which was the boyhood home of Ashe Marson[9] and also (by a curious coincidence) of Psmith, as we learn from the next story.[10] 'Distant' is no doubt a relative term. But Wodehouse could not have meant 'a distant *part* of Shropshire', because we learn that Much Middlefold cannot have been more than fourteen miles from Blandings, and may have been less.[11] No: in *Something Fresh* Blandings is clearly in Wiltshire, because we are told that it is only seventy miles from London[12] (Swindon, where the train made its first stop, is distant seventy-nine miles). It is not until the second page of Leave it to Psmith that we learn that Blandings Castle is in Shropshire. In the interval between Something Fresh and Leave it to Psmith it must have been dismantled brick by brick, together with the village of Market Blandings, and re-erected in Shropshire. Its distance from London gradually increases: in Summer Lightning it is a hundred miles,[13] in Heavy Weather a hundred and fourteen miles,[14] and in Service with a Smile more than a hundred miles.[15] (Bridgnorth, the nearest place in Shropshire to London, is distant one hundred and thirty-five miles.)

Market Blandings was originally five miles from Blandings Castle,[16] but when it was re-erected in Shropshire, the distance shrank to two miles.[17] It stands dreaming the centuries away, a jewel in the green heart of Shropshire. In all England there is no sweeter spot. It is one of the most picturesque little towns in England. It boasts a railway station, a lichened Norman church with a sturdy four-square tower, a decorous High Street, red-roofed shops, age-old inns, a post office, a telephone exchange, a police station, and a Jubilee Memorial watering trough. There are eleven inns at Market Blandings[18] – twelve if you count the distant Cow and Caterpillar on the Shrewsbury Road.[19] Their names are the Wheatsheaf, the Waggoner's Rest, the Beetle and Wedge, the Stitch in Time, the Jolly Cricketers, the Blue Boar, the Blue Cow, the Blue Dragon, the Goat and Feathers, the Goose and Gander and, of course, the Emsworth Arms, which is the most respectable, and serves the best beer,[20] though its cuisine and comfort leave much to be desired.[21] It has a garden sloping down to the river on which rowing boats can be hired.[22] We are not actually told that this river is the Severn, which figures so prominently in the view from Blandings Castle, but it must be, because the Severn receives no tributary large enough for rowing boats in the whole of its course through Shropshire.

There are so many inns in Market Blanding that it must surely once have been a staging post for coaches. Therefore, a main road must run through the town. This road could be any of the following, all of which pass through or start from Shrewsbury: the A.5 from London to Holyhead; the A.49 from Ross-on-Wye to Preston; the A.53 from Shrewsbury to Buxton; the A.458 from Halesowen to Dinas Mawddwy; the A.488 from Cross Gates to Shrewsbury; or the A.526 from Shrewsbury to Wrexham.

Market Blandings has a grocer, a tobacconist, a chemist, an ironmonger, a gentlemen's hairdresser, a doctor,[23] and a firm of house agents. But for more extensive shopping (e.g. for jewellery or ladies' hairdressing) or to go to the dentist one has to go to Shrewsbury. From the Castle Shrewsbury is about three-quarters of an hour's drive by car,[24] i.e. presumably about twenty miles. Shrewsbury is a hundred and fifty-three miles from London, and nine miles west-north-west of the Wrekin.

Between Blandings Castle and Market Blandings is the little hamlet of Blandings Parva, which lies at the gates of the Castle drive and consists of a few cottages, a church, a vicarage, a general store, a duck pond, a filling station (its only concession to modernity), the Blue Boar inn and a school.

At various points in the Saga, neighbouring towns and villages are mentioned. These include Blatchford, Bridgeford, Much Matchingham (the home of Sir Gregory Parsloe-Parsloe), Much Middlefold and Shiffey. Needless to say, these places do not appear in any atlas or gazetteer. But a real place, Bridgnorth, is also mentioned,[25] so Market Blandings cannot have been there.

One of the surest of our certainties is that Market Blandings station is on the main line from Paddington. Many railway journeys between Paddington and Market Blandings are mentioned in the Saga, and some of them are described in detail; but nowhere is there any suggestion that one had to change on to a branch line. This description of the arrival of the 12.50 train from London at Market Blandings station makes it as certain as anything can be not only that the station is on the main line, but also that the London expresses stop there: 'The 12.50 train drew up with a grinding of brakes at the platform of Market Blandings'.[26]

We can now summarise the evidence about the location of Market Blandings:

(i) It is in Shropshire.

(ii) It is about twenty miles from Shrewsbury.

(iii) From Blandings Castle two miles away the Wrekin is in sight.

(iv) The Severn flows through the town.

(v) A main road runs through the town, and leads to Shrewsbury.

(vi) The station is on a G.W.R. main line, and the London expresses stop there.

I must leave it to those better acquainted with Shropshire than I am to choose a place which best fulfils all these conditions. Unless I am much mistaken, there is no such place. In particular, I cannot agree with the critic Usborne's assistant (Colonel Cobb) in *Sunset at Blandings*[27] that Market Blandings is at Buildwas, four miles south of Wellington. Buildwas is not on a main line nor on a main road, and has a ruined twelfth-century abbey; there is no mention of any such abbey at Market Blandings from beginning to end of the Saga.

II. THE RAILWAY[28]

So many railway journeys are mentioned in the Saga that it is not difficult to construct a time-table of the service. Frequently we are told what time a train departs from one station or the other, but not what time it arrives. We should therefore do well to remember that the journey normally takes four hours.[29] If two trains are said to depart from the same station within five minutes of each other, I have conflated them, on the assumption that the discrepancy is a slip on the author's part if it occurs in the same book, and to a retiming of the service if it occurs in different books. We must however remember that the G.W.R. main line timings remained remarkably stable between the two world wars.

Here is the time-table:

Paddington (dep.)	Market Blandings (arr.)	Remarks
08.30[30]	12.30?	
11.15[31]	15.15?	
11.45[32]	15.45?	First stop, Swindon

12.30[33]	16.10[34]	
12.42[35]	16.40[36]	First stop, Swindon
12.50[37]	15.00	
14.00[38]	18.00?	First stop, Swindon
14.15[39]	18.15?	
14.45[40]	18.45	First stop, Oxford
15.00[41]	19.00?	
15.15[42]	19.15?	
16.15[43]	20.15?	First stop, Swindon
17.00[44]	21.10	Restaurant car
18.15?	22.15[45]	
Market Blandings (*dep.*)	*Paddington* (*arr.*)	
08.20[46]	11.50	
08.50[47]	12.00	
10.30[48]	14.30?	
10.50[49]	14.50?	
11.15[50]	15.15?	
12.40[51]	16.40	
14.00[52]	18.00?	
14.15[53]	18.15?	
14.30[54]	18.30?	
15.30[55]	19.30?	
18.00[56]	22.00?	

There are several very odd features about this time-table:

(i) The first thing that must strike the most casual reader is the extreme lavishness of the service – about a dozen trains a day in each direction. He is invited to contrast the real service as it appears in Bradshaw, which is given below.

(ii) In *Leave it to Psmith*, Freddie breaks off an important conversation with Psmith in the Piccadilly Palace Hotel, London, because his father's stern injunction to return to Market Blandings by the 12.50 train is ringing in his ears. He misses it, spends the afternoon in a cinema, and catches the 17.00.[57] Since he was greatly perturbed by the 'disaster' of missing the 12.50, it is strange that he made no attempt to catch any of the six intervening trains.

(iii) In 'Pig-hoo-o-o-o-ey!' we are told that the best train in the day for Market Blandings is the one which leaves Paddington at 14.00: after that there is nothing till 17.05. Even if we assume that '17.05' should read '17.00' (a better documented train), the statement ignores the 14.15, 14.45, 15.00, 15.15 and 16.15.

(iv) In *Heavy Weather*, we are told that the 1445 from Paddington is the only good train in the afternoon, and gets its passengers to Blandings in plenty of time for dinner.[58] This ignores the equally good 14.15 and the even better 12.50, which does the journey in the record time of two hours and ten minutes, and leapfrogs several earlier trains. However, there is a conflict of evidence about this train. Baxter says 'I have had a letter from Miss Halliday. She writes that she is catching the 12.50 train at Paddington, which means that she should arrive at Market Blandings at about three.'[59] But Psmith, who meets Miss Halliday at the station and has to 'while away the time of waiting', tells her 'You have just stepped off the train after a four hour journey, and you are as fresh and blooming as a rose'.[60] So perhaps the Efficient Baxter slipped up for once. Or perhaps, as Usborne suggests, 'three' is a misprint for 'five'.

(v) Even more remarkable is the fact that there appear to be no less than three routes between Paddington and Market Blandings. If it is on the Shrewsbury line, the normal route would be via Bicester, Banbury and Birmingham (Snow Hill), and the train would continue beyond Shrewsbury to Gobowen, Ruabon, Wrexham, Chester and Birkenhead. Yet we are told quite distinctly that one of the trains from London makes Oxford its first stop, and four of them Swindon. Neither Oxford nor Swindon is on the G.W.R. main line to Birmingham and Shrewsbury. However, the route from Paddington to Birmingham did lie through Oxford as late as 1910, before the cut-off link through Bicester was completed. So Wodehouse (who emigrated to America in 1909) did have some excuse for making his trains to Shropshire stop at Oxford. But he had no excuse for making them stop at Swindon. That must be a throw-back to the early days when Blandings Castle was in Wiltshire.

The real service between Paddington and Shrewsbury as shown in Bradshaw for April 1910 is given below. I give the service for Shrewsbury, because I do not know exactly where Market Blandings is. I take it from the 1910 Bradshaw, because this is the nearest edition to the period from 1914 to 1926 (when the Saga took place) to which I have access.

Paddington (dep.)	Shrewsbury (arr.)
00.15	05.05
06.30	12.04
09.50	13.59
11.25	14.53
14.15	17.45
16.55	20.34
19.30	00.03

Shrewsbury (dep.)	Paddington (arr.)
08.09	12.15
10.00	14.08
11.00	15.00
13.33	17.20
14.33	18.20
16.30	20.50
18.30	22.50

I have the following comments on this time-table:

(i) There were seven trains a day in each direction, and not a dozen as the Saga says; and their average timing was four hours ten minutes.

(ii) All the trains passed through Oxford, and most of them stopped there. But when, soon after 1910, the line through Bicester to Banbury was finished, the route through Oxford was abandoned. According to the July 1938 edition of Bradshaw, the service was much the same as in 1910, except that the timings were faster. The average time for the journey was three hours fifty-three minutes.

(iii) Apart from Shrewsbury, the London trains stopped at only two places in Shropshire, Wellington (sometimes) and Gobowen. These places are about eleven and nineteen miles respectively from Shrewsbury. Both are on the A.5, but neither is on the Severn. I do not know Gobowen, but I should be surprised if anyone thought that 'in all England there is no sweeter spot' than Wellington. Our problem therefore remains unresolved.

III. COUSIN GEORGE'S WEDDING

At the beginning of *Heavy Weather*, Ronnie Fish travelled by train from Market Blandings to Norfolk to be best man at the wedding of his cousin George. He left by the 12.40 train[61] (which is one of the trains to London) and returned to Market Blandings at about 19.40 next day by a slower and shabbier train than the 14.45 from London, since 'the festivities connected with his cousin George's wedding and the intricacies of a railway journey across the breadth of England had combined to prevent an earlier return'.[62]

Norfolk is a large county and we are not told in which part of it the wedding took place. Let us suppose it was near Norwich, which, being the county town, has the best communications. The journey must have been indeed an intricate one. There is, of course, more than one route, but assuming that Ronnie chose the best and quickest one, it must have involved no less than four changes and three different railway systems. Thus:

Market Blandings to Birmingham (Snow Hill)	G.W.R.
Birmingham (New Street) to Rugby	L.M.S.
Rugby to Peterborough (East)	L.M.S.
Peterborough (East) to Ely	L.N.E.R.
Ely to Norwich	L.N.E.R.

According to the 1910 edition of Bradshaw, there were only two trains which Ronnie Fish could have caught at Shrewsbury (let alone Market Blandings) and which would have conveyed him to Norwich (let alone some more remote part of Norfolk) in the same day, and two trains back. These were as follows:

Shrewsbury dep.	08.09	10.00
Birmingham (Snow Hill) arr.	09.20	11.12
Birmingham (New Street) dep.	10.05	11.45
Rugby arr.	10.47	12.38
Rugby dep.	11.15	13.05
Peterborough (East) arr.	12.40	15.05
Peterborough (East) dep.	12.52	16.20
Ely arr.	13.38	18.03
Ely dep.	14.06	19.09
Norwich arr.	15.50	20.48

Norwich dep.	07.38	11.10
Ely arr.	09.06	12.48
Ely dep.	09.15	13.00
Peterborough (East) arr.	10.05	13.45
Peterborough (East) dep.	10.15	13.55
Rugby arr.	11.21	15.25
Rugby dep.	11.28	16.01
Birmingham (New Street) arr.	12.11	16.45
Birmingham (Snow Hill) dep.	12.48	17.55
Shrewsbury arr.	13.59	19.10

Obviously, Ronnie could not have caught the 12.40 train from Market Blandings as he said: he must have caught a much earlier train which connected with the 10.00 from Shrewsbury, and so must have arrived at Norwich at 20.48. But when was the wedding? The permitted hours for marriages in 1923 were 08.00 to 15.00 (they were extended to 18.00 in 1934). So the wedding must either have taken place clandestinely and illegally during the night, or else at the unfashionable hour of 09.00 next morning – not later, otherwise Ronnie could not have attended the festivities *and* caught the 11.00 train back to Market Blandings. The latter seems more likely, because the bridegroom's father was a bishop,[63] and surely he should have known the rules.

Confronted by these difficulties, the critic Howarth suggests that King George v may have sent a special train from Sandringham to Market Blandings to convey Ronnie to Norfolk and back. Any suggestion from so eminent a critic is entitled to great respect, even if it is only a conjecture not based on any evidence. But we must regretfully reject this one, for two reasons. First, in *Heavy Weather* Galahad reminds Constance that Ronnie is not 'the Prince of Wales or something'[64] (and that therefore his matrimonial intentions are of no concern to anyone except himself and Sue Brown). Secondly, in early August (when *Heavy Weather* began) King George v would not have been at Sandringham: he would have been racing *Britannia* at Cowes.

NOTES

There are so many editions of all except the most recent of Wode-house's books that we have indicated the date of publication of the editions we have cited. We usually but not always cite the Uniform Autograph edition when it is available; this is indicated by the letter 'A' after the date. The editions referred to were published by Herbert Jenkins, London (to 1968) and Barrie & Jenkins, London (1969 onwards) apart from *Sunset at Blandings* in Part III which was published by Chatto & Windus, London. For the benefit of readers who may be using other editions, we give the chapter number and (if there is one) the section number of all except the most recent books and the Omnibus editions (Jeeves, Golf and Mulliner).

PART I

   AAG – Aunts Aren't Gentlemen (1974)
    BC – Blandings Castle (1957) A
   COJ – Carry On, Jeeves (1960) A
    CW – The Code of the Woosters (1962) A
     IJ – The Inimitable Jeeves (1956) A
    JFS – Jeeves and the Feudal Spirit (1962) A
    JM – Joy in the Morning (1948)
    JO – Jeeves in the Offing (1979)
   MOJ – Much Obliged, Jeeves (1971)
    MS – The Mating Season (1949)
  MTLF – The Man with Two Left Feet (1971)
   RHJ – Right Ho, Jeeves (1957) A
    RJ – Ring for Jeeves (1953)
   SULJ – Stiff Upper Lip, Jeeves (1963)
    TYJ – Thank You, Jeeves (1956) A
    WJ – The World of Jeeves (1967)
   WM – The World of Mr Mulliner (1972)
   YMS – Young Men in Spats (1957) A

Chapter 1

1 WJ p. 176
2 RHJ pp. 186-93 (ch. 22)
3 WJ p. 98
4 JO p. 175 (ch. 17); JFS pp. 36, 153, 174 (chs. 5, 19, 22)
5 WJ p. 45
6 TYJ p. 82 (ch. 9)
7 MTLF p. 26 (ch. 2); WJ p. 326
8 JM p. 11 (ch. 1)
9 WJ pp. 200-1
10 WJ p. 349
11 WJ p. 484
12 WJ pp. 535, 536, 563
13 WJ p. 438
14 MS p. 7 (ch. 1)
15 JM pp. 50, 67-73, 104-5, 135-41, 164, 171 (chs. 7, 9, 10, 16, 17, 20, 21)
16 WJ pp. 8-10, 12-13
17 WJ p. 3; cf. JM p. 12 (ch. 1)
18 WJ p. 8
19 WJ p. 45
20 WJ p. 212
21 WJ p. 213
22 WJ p. 166
23 WJ pp. 228, 239
24 WJ p. 318
25 WJ p. 262
26 RHJ p. 11 (ch. 1)
27 RHJ p. 124 (ch. 13); CW 23 (ch. 2)
28 JO pp. 39-40 (ch. 3)
29 Richard Usborne, *Wodehouse at Work to the End* (Barrie & Jenkins, London, 1977) pp. 182, 185, 187, 189
30 Geoffrey Jaggard, *Wooster's World* (MacDonald & Co, London, 1967) pp. 169-70

Chapter 2

1 MS p. 37 (ch. 4); JO p. 28 (ch. 2); MOJ p. 88
2 WJ pp. 504, 515
3 TYJ p. 55 (ch. 6)
4 P.G. Wodehouse, *Over Seventy* (Herbert Jenkins, London, 1957) p. 54
5 MTLF pp. 28-9
6 MTLF p. 29
7 MTLF pp. 29, 43; WJ 67, 99
8 WJ pp. 14, 16
9 WJ pp. 2, 6
10 WJ p. 5
11 WJ pp. 59, 424, 470, 517; CW p. 10 (ch. 1); MS p. 7 (ch. 1); JM p. 12 (ch. 1); JFS p. 7 (ch. 1); SULJ p. 10 (ch. 1); JO p. 134 (ch. 12); MOJ p. 51
12 JM p. 198 (ch. 24)
13 WJ p. 316
14 WJ p. 438
15 WJ p. 320
16 CW p. 166 (ch. 11)
17 JM p. 11-12 (ch. 1); JFS p. 10 (ch. 1)
18 JM p. 6 (ch. 1). In MOJ pp. 19, 24, Bertie says that Steeple Bumpleigh is in Essex and that it was Aunt Agatha's home during her first marriage: but these are obvious slips
19 MTLF p. 26; WJ p. 326
20 JM p. 95 (ch. 12)
21 JO pp. 109-10 (ch. 10)
22 JM pp. 12, 31 (chs. 1, 4)
23 WJ p. 3
24 JM pp. 193, 245 (chs. 23, 29)
25 JM pp. 109, 240-2 (chs. 14, 28-9)
26 WJ p. 3; JM p. 148 (ch. 18);

JFS p. 103 (ch. 13); MOJ p. 181

27 WJ p. 8
28 JM p. 181 (ch. 22)
29 WJ p. 301
30 WJ p. 482
31 WJ p. 312
32 WJ p. 480
33 MTLF p. 28
34 WJ pp. 471, 481-3
35 Jaggard, *Wooster's World, op. cit.*, pp. 201-2: Geoffrey Jaggard, *Blandings the Blest* (Macdonald & Co., London, 1968) pp. 222-3
36 WJ p. 45
37 WJ p. 513
38 WJ p. 45
39 WJ pp. 211, 213
40 WJ p. 249
41 WJ p. 211
42 WJ pp. 267-8
43 WJ p. 283
44 CW p. 94 (ch. 5) – where she is still Mrs Spenser Gregson
45 JM pp. 11-12 (ch. 1)
46 MS p. 48 (ch. 5) – where she is Agatha Worplesdon
47 WJ pp. 298, 372, 433, 529, 530; RHJ p. 165 (ch. 20); JFS p. 57 (ch. 8); MOJ p. 81
48 WJ p. 301
49 RHJ p. 27 (ch. 3); JFS p. 55 (ch. 8) – 'at her second pop'
50 WJ pp. 298, 369; RHJ p. 27 (ch. 4)
51 CW p. 42 (ch. 3)
52 WJ p. 433
53 WJ p. 372; RHJ pp. 99, 117 (ch. 15)
54 MOJ p. 148
55 WJ pp. 370-1, 487-8; RHJ pp. 44, 47-9 (chs. 6, 7)

56 WJ pp. 433, 435, 442
57 RHJ p. 97 (ch. 12)
58 JFS p. 98 (ch. 13)
59 JFS p. 80 (ch. 11)
60 WJ p. 299
61 RHJ p. 46 (ch. 7); cf. JFS p. 65 (ch. 9)
62 CW p. 14 (ch. 1)
63 RHJ pp. 97, 178 (chs. 12, 21); JFS p. 111 (ch. 14)
64 RHJ p. 179 (ch. 22)
65 JO pp. 10-11 (ch. 1); JFS pp. 81, 148 (chs. 11, 19); SULJ p. 10 (ch. 1)
66 RHJ pp. 96-7 (ch. 12); JFS pp. 93, 111 (chs. 12, 14)
67 WJ p. 70
68 WJ p. 531
69 TYJ p. 100 (ch. 12)
70 WJ pp. 217, 536
71 WJ pp. 517, 545; JO p. 174 (ch. 17); JFS p. 89 (ch. 12); MOJ pp. 14, 101
72 WJ p. 392
73 JFS p. 96 (ch. 13)
74 RHJ p. 179 (ch. 22)
75 WJ p. 286
76 MTLF pp. 26, 28
77 Usborne, *Wodehouse at Work to the End, op. cit.*, p. 193; Jaggard, *Wooster's World, op. cit.*, pp. 189-190
78 COJ p. 174 (ch. 9)
79 WJ p. 300
80 WJ p. 471
81 WJ pp. 468-72
82 WJ pp. 479-80
83 WJ p. 45
84 WJ p. 211
85 WJ p. 45
86 WJ p. 211
87 WJ p. 298
88 *Ante*, chap. 1
89 Usborne, *Wodehouse at*

Work to the End, op. cit., p. 195; Jaggard, *Wooster's World, op. cit.*, p. 164

90 JO p. 56 (ch. 5)
91 JO pp. 88, 204 (chs. 8, 21)
92 WJ p. 558
93 RHJ p. 169 (ch. 20)
94 RHJ p. 184 (ch. 22)
95 WJ pp. 369, 433; RHJ p. 27 (ch. 4)
96 WJ pp. 517, 545; JFS p. 89 (ch. 12); MOJ pp. 14, 101
97 WJ p. 558; cf. JO p. 174 (ch. 17)
98 MOJ p. 51
99 Usborne, *Wodehouse at Work to the End, op. cit.*, p. 195
100 RHJ p. 46 (ch. 7); JO pp. 11, 88 (chs. 1, 8); JFS p. 148 (ch. 19); SULJ p. 11 (ch. 1)
101 WJ p. 484
102 Jaggard, *Wooster's World, op. cit.*, p. 186, maintains that Katherine was a sister of Aunt Agatha and Aunt Dahlia, and cites CW in support; but she does not appear in that work
103 WJ p. 298
104 RHJ p. 179 (ch. 22)
105 RHJ p. 8 (ch. 1)
106 MOJ p. 54
107 WJ pp. 397, 414
108 SULJ pp. 102-3 (ch. 13)
109 JFS p. 81 (ch. 11)
110 WJ p. 536
111 RHJ p. 46 (ch. 7)
112 JFS p. 88 (ch. 12)
113 JFS p. 140 (ch. 18)
114 CW pp. 92-3 (ch. 5)
115 JFS pp. 63-4 (ch. 9)
116 AAG p. 175
117 JFS pp. 62-3 (ch. 9)
118 JFS pp. 65, 80 (chs. 9, 11)
119 JFS pp. 55, 88 (chs. 8, 12)
120 JFS p. 152 (ch. 19)
121 *The Blue Guides: Ireland* Ed. Muirhead, 3rd ed. (Ernest Benn, London, 1962) p. 76

Chapter 3
1 CW p. 69 (ch. 4)
2 Usborne, *Wodehouse at Work to the End, op. cit.*, p. 190; R.B.D. French, *P.G. Wodehouse*, (Oliver & Boyd, Edinburgh and London, 1966) p. 91; Jaggard, *Wooster's World, op. cit.*, p. 191
3 TYJ p. 76 (ch. 9)
4 French, *op. cit.*, p. 91
5 MS p. 155 (ch. 17)
6 JM pp. 23-4 (ch. 3)
7 JM p. 59 (ch. 8)
8 JFS p. 49 (ch. 7)
9 JFS p. 26 (ch. 4)
10 CW pp. 23-4 (ch. 2)
11 RHJ pp. 9, 11 (ch. 1)
12 RJ p. 37 (ch. 4)
13 JFS pp. 138-9 (ch. 18)
14 JO pp. 118, 188-9 (chs. 11, 19)
15 AAG p. 139
16 AAG pp. 111, 121
17 WJ p. 229
18 JM p. 31
19 WJ p. 245; JO pp. 26-8 (ch. 2)
20 WJ p. 209
21 JO p. 26 (ch. 2)
22 WJ p. 516
23 JO p. 26 (ch. 2)
24 WJ p. 107
25 RHJ pp. 137-8 (ch. 17)
26 WJ p. 299

27 WJ pp. 1-2, 5, 17-18; JM p. 15 (ch. 2)
28 WJ pp. 17-18, 350
29 JM p. 11 (ch. 1); JO pp. 124-5 (ch. 11); MOJ pp. 139-40; AAG p. 76; but see JFS p. 99 (ch. 13)
30 WJ p. 318
31 CW p. 51 (ch. 3)
32 WJ p. 279; JM p. 59 (ch. 8); SULJ p. 144 (ch. 19); AAG p. 7
33 CW p. 122 (ch. 8)
34 WJ pp. 356, 541
35 TYJ p. 15 (ch. 1)
36 RHJ p. 15 (ch. 1)
37 WJ p. 342
38 MOJ p. 88
39 WJ pp. 428-9
40 CW p. 45 (ch. 3); but see SULJ p. 96 (ch. 12)
41 MOJ p. 167
42 JO p. 136 (ch. 12)
43 JO p. 49 (ch. 4)
44 MOJ pp. 120-1
45 AAG p. 74; but see RHJ p. 158 (ch. 19); CW p. 141 (ch. 8)
46 JM p. 128 (ch. 16)
47 JM p. 160 (ch. 20)
48 RHJ p. 173 (ch. 21)
49 AAG p. 10
50 WJ p. 166
51 WJ p. 33
52 AAG pp. 60-1

Chapter 4

1 CW p. 12 (ch. 1)
2 WJ pp. 541-2, 561-2; RHJ p. 28 (ch. 4); JO pp. 8, 62-3 (chs. 1, 6); SULJ p. 133 (ch. 17); MOJ pp. 14-15
3 WJ p. 261
4 WJ pp. 260-3; TYJ p. 103 (ch. 12); CW p. 9 (ch. 1)

5 TYJ pp. 56, 103 (chs. 6, 12); RHJ p. 113 (ch. 15)
6 WJ p. 1
7 WJ p. 263
8 RHJ pp. 28, 32 (chs. 4, 5)
9 CW p. 94 (ch. 5)
10 CW p. 7 (ch. 1)
11 TYJ p. 76 (ch. 9)
12 RHJ pp. 186, 188 (ch. 22)
13 WJ p. 408
14 MOJ p. 21
15 WJ pp. 503, 515
16 SULJ p. 127 (ch. 16)
17 WJ p. 343
18 JM pp. 214-22 (ch. 16)
19 RHJ p. 128 (ch. 16)
20 MS pp. 54-63 (ch. 6)
21 MS pp. 44, 46 (ch. 5)
22 MS p. 50 (ch. 5)
23 MS pp. 76-7 (ch. 8)
24 WJ p. 466
25 JO pp. 189-91 (ch. 19)
26 AAG p. 20
27 JFS pp. 11-16 (chs. 1-2)
28 See e.g. MOJ p. 48
29 JO pp. 126, 147 (chs. 12, 14)
30 JFS p. 18 (ch. 2)
31 AAG pp. 45-6
32 RHJ p. 128 (ch. 16)

Chapter 5

1 WJ pp. 495, 497
2 MS p. 145 (ch. 16)
3 MS p. 141 (ch. 16)
4 *Ante*, pp. 21-2
5 JM pp. 23-4 (ch. 3)
6 JM p. 59 (ch. 8)
7 WJ p. 415
8 WJ p. 417
9 WJ p. 325
10 MS p. 155 (ch. 17)
11 WJ p. 353
12 JFS pp. 16-17 (ch. 2); WJ p. 539

13 SULJ p. 30 (ch. 3)
14 WJ p. 481
15 RHJ p. 24 (ch. 3)
16 AAG p. 103
17 WJ p. 484
18 WJ p. 237

Chapter 6

 1 WJ p. 227
 2 YMS p. 75 (No. 5)
 3 WJ p. 508
 4 WJ pp. 20-1, 31
 5 WJ p. 308
 6 TYJ p. 185 (ch. 21)
 7 MS pp. 70, 127 (chs. 7, 14)
 8 AAG p. 44
 9 RHJ p. 38 (ch. 5)
10 CW p. 180 (ch. 12)
11 MS p. 102 (ch. 10)
12 MS p. 91 (ch. 9)
13 JO p. 85 (ch. 8)
14 CW p. 180 (ch. 12)
15 MOJ p. 88
16 MS p. 127 (ch. 14); CW p. 126 (ch. 8)
17 WJ pp. 64-5
18 CW pp. 126, 136 (ch. 8)
19 CW pp. 76-8, 82 (chs. 4, 5)
20 RHJ pp. 43-4 (ch. 6)
21 MS p. 144 (ch. 16)
22 WJ p. 448
23 TYJ p. 62 (ch. 7)
24 Usborne, Wodehouse at Work to the End, op. cit., p. 197
25 For a good example, see JFS pp. 43-4 (ch. 6)
26 CW p. 25 (ch. 2)
27 TYJ p. 58 (ch. 7)
28 JFS pp. 95, 97 (chs. 12, 13)
29 JFS p. 98 (ch. 13)
30 WJ p. 545
31 TYJ p. 44 (ch. 6)
32 TYJ p. 159 (ch. 18)
33 RHJ p. 158 (ch. 19)
34 JM p. 225 (ch. 27)
35 WJ p. 1; JM p. 15 (ch. 2); JFS p. 21 (ch. 3); MOJ pp. 29-30
36 JFS p. 10 (ch. 1)
37 WJ p. 1; JM p. 15 (ch. 2)
38 MOJ p. 19
39 WJ p. 1; JM p. 148 (ch. 18); JFS pp. 103-4 (ch. 13); MOJ p. 181
40 WJ p. 1; JM p. 15 (ch. 2)
41 JFS p. 24 (ch. 3)
42 JM pp. 13, 16-17 (chs. 1, 2)
43 JFS p. 102 (ch. 13)
44 MOJ p. 25
45 WJ p. 3, 17
46 MOJ pp. 26-7
47 JM p. 44 (ch. 6)
48 JM pp. 25, 45 (chs. 3, 6)
49 JFS p. 171 (ch. 22)
50 MOJ p. 27
51 MOJ pp. 19-25
52 JM p. 91 (ch. 12)
53 MOJ p. 92
54 Usborne, Wodehouse at Work to the End op. cit., p. 175; Jaggard, Wooster's World, op. cit., pp. 152, 192
55 WJ p. 69
56 WJ p. 33
57 WJ p. 246
58 WJ p. 350
59 WJ p. 41
60 WJ p. 246
61 WJ p. 350
62 JM p. 14 (ch. 2)
63 WJ pp. 34-5
64 WJ p. 39
65 WJ p. 53
66 WJ p. 245
67 WJ pp. 532, 554, 555

68 WJ p. 55
69 WJ p. 62
70 WJ pp. 65–6
71 IJ pp. 31–2, 37, 40 (ch. 4)
72 WJ pp. 261, 264–6
73 WJ pp. 270–2
74 WJ p. 273
75 WJ pp. 165–7, 170
76 WJ p. 169
77 WJ pp. 178–9
78 WJ p. 398
79 WJ p. 399, 413
80 'Mr Potter Takes a Rest Cure' (BC p. 113)
81 BC p. 114; WJ p. 354; WM p. 246
82 WM p. 232
83 JO p. 112 (ch. 10); WM pp. 230–1, 233, 248
84 WM p. 259
85 JO p. 128 (ch. 12)
86 JO pp. 12, 29 (chs. 1, 3)
87 WJ p. 354
88 JO pp. 191–2 (ch. 19)
89 WJ p. 363
90 WJ pp. 354, 363, 389, 422, 431
91 JO pp. 27–8 (ch. 2)
92 JO pp. 95–6, 127 (chs. 9, 12)
93 BC p. 116; cf. WM pp. 227, 265–6
94 TYJ p. 31 (ch. 4)
95 TYJ p. 58 (ch. 7)
96 TYJ p. 9 (ch. 1)
97 TYJ p. 165 (ch. 19)
98 TYJ p. 31 (ch. 4)
99 TYJ p. 9 (ch. 1)
100 TYJ p. 47 (ch. 6)
101 TYJ p. 47 (ch. 6)
102 TYJ p. 10 (ch. 1)
103 TYJ p. 48 (ch. 6)
104 TYJ pp. 59–60 (ch. 7)
105 RHJ p. 14 (ch. 1)
106 CW pp. 37–8 (ch. 3); SULJ p. 40 (ch. 5)
107 RHJ p. 14 (ch. 1); CW p. 12 (ch. 1); MS p. 38 (ch. 4); SULJ p. 20 (ch. 2)
108 RHJ p. 75 (ch. 10)
109 CW p. 13 (ch. 1); SULJ p. 20 (ch. 2)
110 SULJ p. 97 (ch. 12); MOJ p. 47
111 CW p. 13 (ch. 1); MS p. 38 (ch. 4)
112 MS p. 38 (ch. 4)
113 MS pp. 150–2 (ch. 17)
114 SULJ p. 155 (ch. 20)
115 CW p. 13 (ch. 1).
116 MS p. 10 (ch. 1)
117 RHJ pp. 70, 74–80 (chs. 9, 10).
118 SULJ p. 123 (ch. 15).
119 RHJ p. 169 (ch. 20); CW p. 156 (ch. 10); SULJ pp. 142, 169 (chs. 18, 22); MOJ pp. 145–6.
120 MOJ p. 178
121 SULJ p. 177 (ch. 23)
122 MS p. 13 (ch. 2)
123 MS p. 14 (ch. 2)
124 MS p. 24 (ch. 3)
125 MS p. 108 (ch. 11)
126 AAG p. 9–10
127 AAG p. 64
128 AAG pp. 77, 110–11
129 AAG p. 123
130 TYJ chs. 7–10
131 TYJ pp. 79–80 (ch. 9)
132 WJ p. 347
133 MS pp. 210, 212 (ch. 24)
134 WJ p. 530
135 MOJ p. 117
136 TYJ p. 61 (ch. 7)

Chapter 7

1 WJ pp. 222, 253; AAG p. 7
2 WJ pp. 333, 433, 456, 488; TYJ pp. 21, 70, 148 (chs. 3, 8, 17); RHJ p. 44 (ch. 7);

CW p. 30 (ch. 2); JM pp. 48, 214, 223 (chs. 6, 26); MS pp. 44, 119, 126 (chs. 5, 13, 14); JFS pp. 62, 119, 124 (chs. 9, 15)

3 WJ p. 519; JO p. 29 (ch. 3); SULJ p. 39 (ch. 5); AAG p. 7; MOJ p. 29
4 RHJ p. 45 (ch. 7)
5 TYJ p. 21 (ch. 3)
6 WJ p. 253
7 JM p. 37 (ch. 5)
8 TYJ p. 71 (ch. 8)
9 WJ pp. 505-6
10 WJ p. 514
11 WJ p. 503
12 WJ p. 259
13 JM p. 214 (ch. 26); cf. WJ p. 510
14 MS p. 44 (ch. 5)
15 JM p. 214 (ch. 26)
16 JO p. 115 (ch. 11)
17 WJ p. 222
18 WJ p. 459
19 CW p. 184 (ch. 12)
20 MS pp. 119, 123, 129 (chs. 13, 14)
21 JM p. 85 (ch. 11); JFS p. 119 (ch. 15)
22 WJ p. 276
23 WJ pp. 266-7
24 WJ pp. 268-71
25 WJ pp. 274-6
26 WJ pp. 265-6
27 CW p. 8 (ch. 1)
28 JO pp. 115-16 (ch. 11)
29 WJ p. 87
30 JFS p. 35 (ch. 5)
31 CW p. 94 (ch. 5)
32 WJ p. 19

Chapter 8

1 WJ pp. 18, 95-6
2 WJ p. 315
3 RHJ p. 200 (ch. 23)
4 WJ pp. 66, 111, 224, 431; SULJ pp. 188-9 (ch. 24)
5 RHJ p. 175 (ch. 21)
6 RHJ p. 200 (ch. 23)
7 RJ p. 39 (ch. 4)
8 cf. WJ p. 122
9 RHJ p. 20 (ch. 2)
10 WJ pp. 4, 18
11 WJ pp. 55-6, 66
12 WJ pp. 83, 95-6
13 WJ pp. 97, 98-9, 101, 105, 111-12
14 WJ pp. 212, 224
15 WJ pp. 296, 315
16 WJ pp. 416, 417, 431
17 RHJ pp. 14-16, 20, 25-6, 50, 63-4, 175, 200 (chs. 1-3, 7, 9, 21, 23)
18 SULJ pp. 15-16, 188-9 (chs. 1, 24)

Chapter 9

1 WJ p. 133
2 WJ pp. 352-3
3 WJ p. 493
4 TYJ p. 89 (ch. 10)
5 TYJ p. 110 (ch. 13)
6 WJ p. 47
7 TYJ p. 13 (ch. 1); CW p. 22 (ch. 2); JO p. 28 (ch. 2)
8 TYJ pp. 9-12 (ch. 1)
9 TYJ p. 153 (ch. 17)
10 TYJ pp. 106-7, 130, 141-7 (chs. 12, 15, 16); WJ p. 532
11 WJ pp. 542-5
12 e.g. CW p. 94 (ch. 5); JO p. 56 (ch. 5)
13 JO pp. 8-9 (chap. 1)
14 JO pp. 41-2, 105 (chs. 3, 4, 10)
15 JO pp. 108, 147-8 (chs. 10, 14)
16 JO pp. 107-8 (ch. 10)

Chapter 10

1 JFS p. 63 (ch. 9); JO p. 7 (ch. 1)
2 TYJ pp. 15, 57 (chs. 2, 6)
3 MS p. 17 (ch. 2)
4 MS p. 16 (ch. 2)
5 MS p. 68 (ch. 7)
6 MS pp. 19–20 (ch. 2)
7 MS p. 44 (ch. 5)
8 MS pp. 62–5 (ch. 6)
9 MS pp. 67–8 (chs. 6–7)
10 MS pp. 74, 78 (chs. 7–8)
11 MS pp. 119, 123, 129 (chs. 13–14)
12 MS p. 215 (ch. 24)
13 MS pp. 133–4 (ch. 15)
14 MS p. 156 (ch. 18)
15 MS p. 193 (ch. 22)
16 MS pp. 133–4 (ch. 15)
17 MS pp. 141, 143 (ch. 16)
18 MS pp. 149–52 (ch. 17)
19 MS p. 155 (ch. 17)
20 MS pp. 156–7, 168 (chs. 18, 20)
21 MS p. 57 (ch. 6)
22 MS p. 123 (ch. 13)

PART II

GO – The Golf Omnibus (1973)
WJ – The World of Jeeves (1967)
WM – The World of Mr Mulliner (1972)

Chapter 11

1 GO p. 445
2 GO pp. 56, 131, 227, 356
3 GO p. 105
4 GO pp. 413, 416, 443
5 GO pp. 73, 335
6 GO p. 255
7 GO p. 324
8 GO p. 444
9 GO p. 234
10 GO pp. 56–8
11 GO pp. 96–104
12 GO pp. 108–17, 327, 329–337, 435–8, 449–50
13 GO p. 323
14 GO pp. 209, 291–2
15 GO pp. 25, 37, 65, 91, 209, 273, 291, 443 (but see 177, 397, where the terrace overlooks the 18th green)
16 GO pp. 119–20
17 GO p. 121
18 GO pp. 230, 266; cf. 77
19 GO pp. 324–5
20 GO p. 91
21 GO p. 80
22 GO p. 92
23 GO p. 228
24 WJ p. 281
25 Note 15, *supra*
26 GO pp. 25, 43, 86, 98, 198, 217, 238, 248, 291, 314, 330, 422
27 GO pp. 444–5
28 GO p. 430
29 GO p. 308
30 GO p. 378
31 GO p. 452
32 GO p. 378
33 GO p. 308
34 GO p. 315; cf. 437
35 GO p. 444
36 GO pp. 378–9
37 GO p. 308
38 GO p. 316

39 GO p. 446
40 GO p. 308
41 GO p. 308
42 GO pp. 430, 444
43 GO p. 435
44 GO p. 459
45 GO p. 462
46 GO p. 308
47 GO p. 452
48 GO p. 378

49 GO p. 448
50 GO p. 308
51 GO p. 445
52 GO p. 378
53 GO p. 436
54 GO p. 378; cf. pp. 445, 463
55 GO p. 308
56 GO pp. 309, 315, 320
57 GO pp. 382, 430, 446, 462–4
58 WM p. 77

PART III

BC – Blandings Castle (1957) A
FM – Full Moon (1947)
GB – Galahad at Blandings (1965)
HW – Heavy Weather (1933)
LEO – Lord Emsworth and Others (1956) A
LIP – Leave it to Psmith (1961) A
NS – Nothing Serious (1950)
PB – A Pelican at Blandings (1969)
PHW – Pigs Have Wings (1952)
PP – Plum Pie (1966)
SB – Sunset at Blandings (1977)
SF – Something Fresh (1969)
SL – Summer Lightning (1929)
SS – Service with a Smile (1962)
UFS – Uncle Fred in the Springtime (1962) A

Chapter 12
1 PHW p. 216 (ch. 11.5)
2 SF, Preface; BC, Preface
3 SF p. 84 (ch. 5.2)
4 BC, Preface
5 LIP p. 8 (ch. 1.1). (The story begins on June 30 and ends 8 or 9 days later.)
6 LIP p. 150 (ch. 9.6)
7 LIP p. 207 (ch. 13.1)
8 SL p. 21 (ch. 1.2)
9 HW p. 307 (ch. 17)
10 SL p. 37 (ch. 1.4)
11 HW p. 307 (ch. 17)
12 HW pp. 28, 91, 286 (chs. 2, 6, 16)
13 SL p. 297 (ch. 17)
14 HW p. 46 (ch. 3)
15 SL pp. 70, 294 (chs. 3.1, 17)
16 SL p. 302 (ch. 18); HW pp. 41, 47 (ch. 3)
17 BC, Preface
18 LEO p. 12
19 LEO pp. 13, 16, 20, 27, 42

20 LEO p. 30

21 UFS pp. 121, 124 (chs. 12, 13)

22 UFS p. 23 (ch. 2)

23 FM p. 138 (ch. 7.1)

24 FM pp. 63, 80, 176 (chs. 3.7, 4.4, 8.1)

25 FM p. 171 (ch. 8.1)

26 SL p. 31 (ch. 1.3)

27 BC p. 99 (No. 6)

28 FM pp. 7, 202 (chs. 1.1, 9.2)

29 FM p. 165 (ch. 7.6)

30 PHW pp. 29, 37, 219 (chs. 1.5, 2.2, 11.6)

31 SS pp. 7, 44, 192 (chs. 1.1, 3.1, 12)

32 SS p. 66 (ch. 4.3)

33 SL p. 161 (ch. 8)

34 SS p. 182 (ch. 12)

35 SS p. 7 (ch. 1.1)

36 GB pp. 16, 21 (chs. 1.2, 2.1)

37 GB pp. 22, 89 (chs. 2.1, 6.1)

38 GB p. 17 (ch. 1.2)

39 GB pp. 7–8 (ch. 1.2)

40 GB p. 42 (ch. 3.2)

41 GB p. 170 (ch. 10.1)

42 GB pp. 192, 208 (chs. 11.2, 12.1)

43 PB p. 7

44 PB p. 164

45 PB p. 5

46 PB p. 54

47 SB p. 19

48 SB pp. 35–7

49 SF p. 43 (ch. 3.2)

50 SL p. 91 (ch. 3.5); HW pp. 33, 82, 286 (chs. 3, 6, 16); BC pp. 27, 58 (Nos. 2, 3); LEO pp. 50, 51; PHW p. 18 (ch. 1.3); SS p. 111 (ch. 7.2); GB p. 138 (ch. 8.3); PP p. 80

51 SF p. 37 (ch. 3.1)

52 LIP p. 188 (ch. 11.4)

53 LIP p. 51 (ch. 4)

54 LIP p. 178 (ch. 11.1)

55 LIP p. 230 (ch. 14)

56 HW pp. 46, 50 (chs. 3, 4); FM p. 63 (ch. 3.7)

57 HW p. 194 (ch. 10)

58 PHW p. 21 (ch. 1.4); GB p. 185 (ch. 11.1)

59 PHW p. 89 (ch. 4.3)

60 SL p. 25 (ch. 1.2); FM p. 63 (ch. 3.7); GB p. 23 (ch. 2.1)

61 SL p. 28 (ch. 1.2)

62 SL pp. 84, 172 (chs. 3.4, 8); HW pp. 58, 304–5 (chs. 4, 17); FM pp. 147–8 (ch. 7.3); PHW pp. 86, 110, 207 (chs. 4.3, 5.2, 11.2); GB p. 203 (ch. 11.3)

63 SL pp. 142–3 (ch. 7.1)

64 SL p. 28 (ch. 1.2)

65 SL pp. 83, 148 (chs. 3.4, 7.2)

66 SL p. 305 (ch. 18)

67 HW pp. 55–6 (ch. 4); GB p. 137 (ch. 8.3)

68 HW p. 195 (ch. 10)

69 HW p. 119 (ch. 7)

70 HW p. 198 (ch. 10)

71 HW p. 206 (ch. 10)

72 SL p. 310 (ch. 18)

73 FM p. 64 (ch. 3.7)

74 SL p. 310 (ch. 18)

75 SL p. 309 (ch. 18); HW pp. 204–5 (ch. 10)

76 HW pp. 58–60 (ch. 4)

77 HW p. 86 (ch. 6)

78 HW p. 206 (ch. 10)

79 SL p. 123 (ch. 4.3)

80 HW p. 45 (ch. 3)

81 GB p. 180 (ch. 10.3)

82 SL p. 167 (ch. 8)

83 GB p. 17 (ch. 1.2)

Chapter 13

1 *Ante*, pp. 90–1, 95

2 SL p. 123 (ch. 4.3)

3 HW p. 86 (ch. 6)
4 HW p. 206 (ch. 10)
5 HW pp. 203-4 (ch. 10)
6 HW p. 310 (ch. 18)
7 HW pp. 84-9 (ch. 6)
8 HW p. 206 (ch. 10)
9 PHW p. 216 (ch. 11.5)

Chapter 14
1 *Ante*, p. 95
2 BC p. 67 (No. 4)
3 SF p. 37 (ch. 3.1)
4 LIP p. 69 (ch. 6.3)
5 SL p. 254 (ch. 13.3)
6 SL p. 297 (ch. 17)
7 GB p. 51 (ch. 3.4)
8 PHW p. 100 (ch. 5.2)
9 SL p. 310 (ch. 18)
10 SB p. 26
11 HW p. 296 (ch. 17); PP p. 88
12 LIP p. 113 (ch. 8.4)
13 GB p. 17 (ch. 1.2); NS p. 188
14 BC pp. 27, 37, 41 (No. 2)
15 LIP p. 238 (ch. 14); BC p. 14 (No. 1)
16 BC p. 26 (No. 1)
17 SF pp. 23-4 (ch. 2.1); LIP p. 9 (ch. 1.1)
18 SF p. 45 (ch. 3.3)
19 SF p. 183 (ch. 10.3)
20 SF pp. 180-2 (ch. 10.3)
21 LIP p. 25 (ch. 1.3)
22 LIP pp. 21-2, 239 (chs. 1.3, 14); UFS p. 139 (ch. 14)
23 SF pp. 82, 130 (chs. 5.1, 7.1)
24 SF pp. 160-1, (ch. 9.3)
25 LIP p. 150 (ch. 9.6)
26 SS p. 182 (ch. 12)
27 BC pp. 44-7 (No. 3)
28 LEO pp. 13-16
29 SL pp. 31-4 (ch. 1.3)
30 LIP pp. 17-18 (ch. 1.2)
31 SL pp. 305-11 (ch. 18); HW pp. 45, 300-4 (chs. 3, 17)
32 UFS p. 27 (ch. 2)
33 SL p. 306 (ch. 18)
34 UFS p. 207 (ch. 20)
35 UFS p. 76 (ch. 8)
36 UFS pp. 201-6 (ch. 20). Astonishingly, both the critic Usborne (*Wodehouse at Work to the End, op. cit.*, 118) and the critic Jaggard (*Blandings the Blest, op. cit.* 205,) attribute this assertion to Galahad. He would never have done such a thing: he was much too fond of Clarence.
37 SS pp. 34-6 (ch. 2.2)
38 SS pp. 150, 156-60 (ch. 10.1, 10.2)
39 GB p. 17 (ch. 1.2)
40 FM p. 12 (ch. 1.2); GB p. 28 (ch. 2.2)
41 GB p. 53 (ch. 3.4)
42 GB p. 52 (ch. 3.4)
43 GB pp. 222-4 (ch. 12.3)
44 SB p. 62
45 LIP pp. 230-1 (ch. 14)
46 SF p. 154 (ch. 9.1)
47 LEO pp. 9-11
48 SL pp. 30-1, 41, 70-6 (chs. 1.2, 1.5, 3.1, 3.2)
49 UFS pp. 106-7 (ch. 11)
50 LIP p. 178 (ch. 11.1)
51 LEO p. 10
52 SL pp. 41, 70-6 (chs. 1.5, 3.1, 3.2)
53 SL p. 306 (ch. 18)
54 GB p. 84 (ch. 6.1)
55 LIP pp. 237-9 (ch. 14)
56 HW p. 109 (ch. 7)
57 SL p. 293 (ch. 17)
58 HW pp. 48-9 (ch. 3)
59 HW pp. 217, 220 (ch. 11)
60 PHW p. 84 (ch. 4.2)
61 BC p. 28, (No. 2)

62 SS p. 92 (ch. 6.3)

63 SS pp. 7, 35 (chs. 1.1, 2.2)

64 SS p. 35 (ch. 2.2)

65 SS p. 91 (ch. 6.3)

66 GB pp. 223–4 (ch. 12.3)

67 GB p. 84 (ch. 6.1)

68 SL p. 22 (ch. 1.2); PHW pp. 70–1 (ch. 3.2)

69 SL p. 23 (ch. 1.2)

70 GB p. 185 (ch. 11.1)

71 GB p. 73 (ch. 5.1)

72 SL p. 82 (ch. 3.4); PHW p. 40 (ch. 2.3)

73 SS pp. 10, 11 (ch. 1.1); GB p. 127 (ch. 8.2); cf. PHW p. 41 (ch. 2.3), where the political discussion is said to have taken place in the Emsworth Arms

74 PHW p. 98 (ch. 5.1)

75 GB p. 128 (ch. 8.2)

76 PHW p. 116 (ch. 5.5)

77 BC pp. 64–5 (No. 4). This is confirmed by PHW p. 8 (ch. 1.1) ('two years ago')

78 SL p. 21 (ch. 1.2)

79 SS p. 8 (ch. 1.1)

80 SS p. 91 (ch. 6.3)

81 SS p. 179 (ch. 11.3)

82 GB pp. 127, 218 (chs. 8.2, 12.3)

83 SL p. 22 (ch. 1.2)

84 UFS p. 127 (ch. 13)

85 HW p. 40 (ch. 3)

86 HW pp. 125–8, 295–6 (chs. 7, 17)

87 HW p. 126 (ch. 7)

88 PHW p. 14 (ch. 1.3)

89 FM p. 173 (ch. 8.1)

90 FM pp. 231, 232 (ch. 10.5)

91 PHW p. 14 (ch. 1.3)

92 PHW pp. 14, 16–17, 49 (chs. 1.3, 2.4)

93 LEO p. 15

94 PHW pp. 50–1 (chs. 2.4, 2.5)

95 PHW pp. 14, 16 (ch. 1.3)

96 PHW p. 215 (ch. 11.4); GB p. 89 (ch. 6.1)

97 GB p. 214 (ch. 12.2)

98 PB p. 159

99 FM pp. 7–8 (ch. 1.1)

100 SL pp. 89–93, 223–34, 234–5, 263–4, 280 (chs. 3.5, 3.6, 12.2, 12.4, 13.3, 15)

101 HW pp. 289–92, 304–5, 310 (chs. 16, 17, 18)

102 UFS pp. 134, 176–7, 181, 192, 194 (chs. 13, 18, 19)

103 FM pp. 149–50, 167 (chs. 7.3, 7.6)

104 PHW pp. 121–2, 196–7 (chs. 5.6, 10.3)

105 GB pp. 68, 103–4 (chs. 4.2, 7.2). He was Whiffle again in PB p. 159 and SB pp. 83, 91

106 LEO pp. 13, 20

107 PHW pp. 9–10, 14, 215 (chs. 1.1, 1.2, 11.4); SS pp. 10–11 (ch. 1.1)

108 GB pp. 89, 218 (chs. 6.1, 12.3). The diet increased again to 57,000 calories in PB p. 12 but was reduced to 5,700 in SB p. 81

Chapter 15

1 FM p. 14 (ch. 1.2); PHW pp. 15, 85 (chs. 1.3, 4.3)

2 FM p. 63 (ch. 3.7); PHW p. 15 (ch. 1.3); GB pp. 22–3 (ch. 2.1)

3 PHW pp. 22–3 (ch. 1.4)

4 HW pp. 46, 50 (chs. 3, 4); FM p. 63 (ch. 3.7)

5 PHW p. 89 (ch. 4.3)

6 SL p. 200 (ch. 11.1); PHW p. 207 (ch. 11.2)

7 SL p. 200 (ch. 11.1); GB p. 88 (ch. 6.1)
8 FM p. 241 (ch. 10.5); PHW p. 24 (ch. 1.4); GB p. 48 (ch. 3.4)
9 GB pp. 88-9 (ch. 6.1)
10 SL p. 26 (ch. 1.2); GB p. 23 (ch. 2.1)
11 SL p. 27 (ch. 1.2); HW p. 50 (ch. 4); PHW p. 15 (ch. 1.3); GB p. 29 (ch. 1.2)
12 HW p. 50 (ch. 4)
13 FM p. 63 (ch. 3.7); GB p. 34 (ch. 3.1)
14 SL p. 24 (ch. 1.2); HW pp. 9-10 (ch. 1)
15 HW pp. 116-19, 195, 198 (chs. 7, 10)
16 SL p. 149 (ch. 7.2)
17 HW pp. 156-8 (ch. 8)
18 HW p. 249 (ch. 14)
19 SL p. 145 (ch. 7.2)
20 PHW p. 86 (ch. 4.3)
21 HW pp. 116-17 (ch. 7); PHW p. 86 (ch. 4.3)
22 HW p. 117 (ch. 7)
23 PHW p. 86 (ch. 4.3)
24 HW pp. 116-19 (ch. 7)
25 FM p. 67 (ch. 3.7)
26 PHW pp. 85-6 (ch. 4.3)
27 PHW p. 176 (ch. 9.2)
28 PHW pp. 183-4 (ch. 10.1)
29 FM pp. 186-7 (ch. 8.2); GB p. 54 (ch. 3.4)
30 PHW p. 31 (ch. 1.5); GB pp. 213-14 (ch. 12.2)
31 HW pp. 201-7 (ch. 10)
32 HW pp. 300-3 (ch. 17)
33 SL pp. 146-150 (ch. 7.2); PHW pp. 36-8 (ch. 2.2)
34 FM pp. 195, 197-9 (ch. 9.1)
35 HW pp. 192-201 (ch. 10)
36 HW pp. 107 (ch. 7)
37 HW p. 200 (ch. 10)

38 FM p. 133 (ch. 6.6)
39 FM pp. 130-1 (ch. 6.6); PB p. 18
40 GB p. 57 (ch. 4.1)
41 GB p. 31 (ch. 2.3)
42 FM pp. 65-8, 101-3, 136-7 (chs. 3.7, 5.3, 6.6)
43 FM pp. 94-6, 123, 131-2, 189-90 (chs. 5.2, 6.4, 6.6, 8.2)
44 HW p. 121 (ch. 7)
45 SL pp. 314-16 (ch. 19)

Chapter 16

1 See the Threepwood family tree, *ante*, p. 104-5
2 This refers to the legal power (very rarely exercised) enjoyed by the eldest son and heir of refusing to take part in a resettlement of the family estates when he attained twenty-one
3 *The Land Laws*, p. 9
4 FM p. 133 (ch. 6.6)
5 PHW p. 22 (ch. 1.4)
6 SF pp. 180-2 (ch. 10.3)
7 LIP p. 25 (ch. 1.3)
8 SF pp. 23-4 (ch. 2.1); LIP pp. 8-9 (ch. 1.1)
9 SL p. 123 (ch. 4.3)
10 SL p. 48 (ch. 2.2)
11 SL pp. 232, 234, 282-3, 284, 293 (chs. 12.4, 15, 17)
12 SL pp. 282-3 (ch. 15)

Chapter 17

1 LIP p. 8 (ch. 1.1); GB p. 20 (ch. 2.1)
2 SF p. 167 (ch. 10.1); LIP p. 119 (ch. 8.6)
3 SL p. 190 (ch. 10.2)
4 SL p. 273 (ch. 14.2)

5   SF p. 88 (ch. 5.3)
6   LIP p. 8 (ch. 1.1)
7   LIP pp. 185–6 (ch. 11.3)
8   GB p. 21 (ch. 2.1)
9   SF p. 87 (ch. 5.2)
10 LIP p. 238 (ch. 14)
11 LIP p. 217 (ch. 13.3)
12 SF p. 42 (ch. 3.2)
13 SL p. 59 (ch. 2.2)
14 HW p. 117 (ch. 7)
15 SS p. 40 (ch. 2.3)
16 SF p. 144 (ch. 8.2)
17 LIP p. 93 (ch. 7.3); HW p. 146 (ch. 8); UFS p. 90 (ch. 9); FM p. 76 (ch. 4.2); GB p. 72 (ch. 5.1)
18 SF p. 135 (ch. 7.2)
19 BC p. 92 (No. 5)
20 SF p. 135 (ch. 7.2); HW p. 281 (ch. 16); UFS pp. 207, 218 (chs. 14, 15); GB p. 106 (ch. 7.2)
21 HW pp. 259–62 (ch. 15); PHW pp. 175–6 (ch. 9.2); PB p. 132
22 HW p. 147 (ch. 8); UFS p. 154 (ch. 15); SS p. 123 (ch. 8.2); GB p. 105 (ch. 7.2)
23 The vet, so often summoned to the Castle to minister to the Empress, lived at Much Matchingham: HW p. 255
24 FM p. 166 (ch. 7.6)
25 FM p. 137 (ch. 6.6); PHW p. 101 (ch. 5.2); GB p. 46 (ch. 3.3); PB p. 166
26 LIP p. 106 (ch. 8.3)
27 SB pp. 192–6
28 This and the succeeding section were first written two years before Usborne's appendix on the trains was published in SB pp. 187–99. Four trains in my list (the

12.30 and 15.00 from Paddington and the 14.15 and 15.30 from Market Blandings) do not appear in Usborne's

29 SF, Preface; LIP p. 106 (ch. 8.3); HW p. 70 (ch. 5); FM p. 180 (ch. 8.2) (contrast *ib.* 69 (ch. 4.1), 3 hours 40 minutes)
30 SB p. 99
31 HW p. 114 (ch. 7); PB p. 29
32 SS pp. 36, 41, 153 (chs. 2.2, 3.1, 10.2)
33 SS pp. 122, 133 (chs. 8.2, 9.2)
34 SS p. 148 (ch. 10.1); GB p. 143 (ch. 9.1)
35 FM pp. 60, 69, 137, 163 (chs. 3.6, 4.1, 6.6, 7.6)
36 SL p. 161 (ch. 8)
37 LIP pp. 28, 87, 99 (chs. 1.5, 7.2, 8.1)
38 BC p. 54 (No. 3)
39 SL p. 134 (ch. 6)
40 HW pp. 44, 61, 70–1 (chs. 3, 4, 5); UFS pp. 18, 74 (chs. 2, 8); PB p. 78 (1433)
41 SF p. 28 (ch. 2.2)
42 BC p. 66 (No. 4)
43 SF pp. 77, 83, 84 (ch. 5.1)
44 LIP p. 82 (ch. 7.1); BC p. 60 (No. 3); UFS pp. 73, 123, 196 (chs. 7, 13, 19)
45 PHW p. 186 (ch. 10.1)
46 UFS pp. 80, 108 (chs. 8, 11)
47 HW p. 61 (ch. 4)
48 SL p. 95 (ch. 3.7); SS pp. 9, 176 (chs. 1.1, 11.2)
49 SF p. 184 (ch. 10.3)
50 SL p. 24 (ch. 1.2)
51 FM pp. 125, 130 (chs. 6.5, 6.6)
52 BC p. 49 (No. 3); UFS p. 29 (ch. 2)

53 SS p. 110 (ch. 7.3)
54 LIP p. 10 (ch. 1.1)
55 SL p. 14 (ch. 1.1)
56 FM p. 88 (ch. 5.1)
57 LIP pp. 65-7, 87 (chs. 6.2, 7.2)
58 HW p. 44 (ch. 3)

59 LIP p. 99 (ch. 8.1)
60 LIP p. 106 (ch. 8.3)
61 HW p. 32 (ch. 3)
62 HW p. 79 (ch. 6)
63 HW p. 57 (ch. 4)
64 HW p. 301 (ch. 17)

INDEX